My Irish Chil…

Maureen Penn

ISBN: 978-0-473-48618-1
Book design and print by BookPrint Ltd
Cover photographs:
Author standing by the Mall in Westport in 2003
Author aged five outside O'Malleys on the Mall c1937

I dedicate this book to my mother
Margaret Noone and to my Nan
Margaret McDermott

Contents

CHAPTER ONE

Up To My Birth

My name is Maureen Penn. I was born Mary Christina Noone on the 21st of December 1932 in Ballina, a town in County Mayo on the west coast of the Republic of Ireland. I am now 86 years old. I am writing my story in New Zealand where I have lived since 1954.

County Mayo is in the province of Connaught. Connaught is the wildest of Ireland's four provinces and Mayo is the wildest county in Connaught. It was here, where the soil is poor and the terrain most rugged, that the Irish suffered the most during the Great Famine, between 1846 and 1850. In 1838, the English divided Ireland into Poor Law Unions. A workhouse was built in each union to house the destitute poor. The purpose of the workhouse was to provide basic food and shelter and to make the workhouse experience so unpleasant that the destitute would avoid it at all cost. My mother's sister, Bridget (Bidney) was born in the Ballina Union Workhouse in 1908. My mother (Mammy) was born in the Ballina Union Workhouse on 29th August 1910. I have been able to trace back as far as my Nan's grandfather, Patrick Barrett. Patrick's son, (Nan's father) was Michael

Barrett. It seems Michael was most likely from Carrowleagh, northeast of Rehins, which is where Michael moved to and married Anne McHale in 1872. Rehins is just south of the town of Ballina, between Lough (Lake) Conn on its west side and the River Moy to the east. There is a place called Knockmore in this area and this was the place where many of my ancestors' baptisms took place.

Michael and Anne Barrett had seven children. The eldest was my grandmother, Margaret Barrett (Nan). You will soon discover, as you read my story, that my grandmother was an extraordinary character; courageous, disrespectful of authority and – judged against the standards of the time – immoral. I loved my Nan and she loved and protected me.

Nan was baptised in 1873. After Nan came Patrick, in 1875. It seems he died in his twenties. After Patrick came my great-uncle Anthony in 1877. He was killed in 1914, within a month of arriving in Flanders. After Anthony was my great-uncle Robert, born in 1879. Robert survived the war but died in 1923 aged only 44 years. After Robert came my great-uncle William, in 1881. He survived the war but was wounded and Nan looked after him. I knew William as 'Uncle Billy'. Before or after Uncle Billy came Thomas and the youngest was Mary. I don't know anything about Thomas or Mary, and in fact I wasn't aware of either of them, or Patrick, until I started my research.

I return now to my Nan. Nan was baptised on the 6th of July 1873 in Behybane Parish.

The Census of Ireland conducted on Sunday, 31st of March 1901 has Nan aged 25 living with her mother, Anne Barrett, in Abbey Street, Ballina. Abbey Street is in the suburb of

Ardnaree. They moved to Ardnaree in 1881 or 1882. My great-grandfather, Michael Barrett, died before January 1898, from which time all rent demands were made to Anne. The Census entry reads;

Anne Barrett	*Head of Family*	*Roman Catholic*	*Cannot read*	*60 years*	*Widow*
Maggy Barrett	*Daughter*	*Roman Catholic*	*Cannot read*	*25 years*	*Servant*
Robert Barrett	*Son*	*Roman Catholic*	*Cannot read*	*22 years*	*Labourer*
William Barrett	*Son*	*Roman Catholic*	*Cannot read*	*21 years*	*Labourer*
Thomas Barrett	*Son*	*Roman Catholic*	*Cannot read*	*20 years*	*Labourer*

The next official record I have of my Nan is Mammy's birth certificate. Nan named her daughter after herself, Margaret Barrett. Mammy was born in the workhouse on the 29th of August 1910. Mammy was illegitimate. She was the best mother anybody could have.

Nan would have been 34 when she had Bidney and 37 when she had Mammy. I do not know if Bidney and Mammy had the same father.

In the 1911 Census, Mammy and Bidney are both recorded as living in the Workhouse. I have assumed Nan was with them in the Workhouse because Mammy was only 7 months old, but Nan is not recorded in the Census at all.

The 1911 Census shows that as Nan and her two babies

are in the Workhouse, her three brothers (Anthony, William and Robert) are living just down the road in a house in Chapel Lane. The Census shows that none of the three brothers can read, all of them are single and all are general labourers.

I ask myself how Nan's three brothers could have allowed her and her babies to be taken into the Workhouse. Were the brothers too poor to support their sister and nieces? Was the Chapel Lane house too small? Were they ashamed of Nan for having not one but two children out of wedlock? Was my Nan shunned by others in the town? Perhaps my brothers could not afford in this Catholic town to have been connected with her.

The next record I have is the Scoil Chroí Íosa (roll call) of the Convent of Mercy Girls' Primary School. Mammy is recorded in the Roll Call as 'Maggy Barrett' from Ardnaree in 1914. I don't know when Nan got out of the Workhouse or where she was living when Mammy was going to school.

On 14th May 1916, the daughter of Nan and James McDermott was born. Her name was Maria Anna. She was always called Mamie. Nearly two years later, on 6th March 1918, Nan married Mamie's father, James. Bidney would have been ten years old at that time and Mammy seven years old. Nan and James' marriage certificate states that James McDermott was a Bachelor from Ardnaree aged 30 and that Margaret Barrett, a Spinster also from Ardnaree was aged 34. James McDermott signed his name but Nan signed an "X". So not only could Nan not read and write, she couldn't even sign her own name. Nan and James McDermott went on to have a son, John McDermott.

Nan's Baptism Certificate states she was baptised on 6th July 1873 so, assuming that date is her birthdate, she would have been 44, not 34 at the date of her marriage. It seems extraordinary that Nan would have pretended to have been ten years younger than she was. She had lived in Ballina for 20 years so people must have known how old she was. James McDermott and his parents had all lived in Ardnaree for many years so they must have all known Nan was14 years older than him. I wonder whether the '34' instead of '44' was a mistake that nobody noticed.

At some point, James McDermott and Nan and their four children rented a house at 60 Healy Terrace in Ballina. I don't know much about Mammy's life over the next few years.

These were turbulent years in Ireland. From 1919 to 1921 the Irish people waged a War of Independence against the British. This led to the signing of the Treaty on the 6th of December 1921. The Treaty and the subsequent general election led to the formation of the Irish Free State in 1922. The IRA opposed the Treaty and Ireland endured a Civil War from mid 1922 to mid 1923. I think most of the action took place in Dublin and other areas but it would still have been a dangerous and unsettling atmosphere for Mammy as she entered her teenage years.

The next thing I know is that Mammy left Ballina in about 1930, aged 20, and moved to Westport, a picturesque town on the Carrowbeg River, 35 miles from Ballina. I don't know why Mammy left Ballina, or why she chose Westport. She came to work as a servant for the O'Malleys and she moved into their house. Mr O'Malley was a builder. He and his wife had six children. Mammy's job was to get the children up in the morning, get them ready for school, do their washing and all the other jobs. The O'Malley's house was on the Mall, just a couple of doors away from the post office.

It was in Westport that Mammy met my father, James Noone. My father was born in Galway on the 10th of November 1901 so when Mammy, aged 20, moved to Westport, Dad was aged 29 years.

Dad's parents (Tom Noone and Mary (Heraty)) were from Galway. They were each born in 1877.

In the March 1911 Census, the Noones were all living in High Street. I believe they would have been living in the house on the corner of High Street and St John's Row. It is a stone's throw from the house I grew up in, on High Street.

The Mall, Westport

The family is recorded as:

Thomas Noone	*Age 43*
Mary Noone	*Age 40*
Martin	*Age 18*
Thomas	*Age 14*
James (Dad)	*Age 9 ("scholar")*
Katie	*Age 6*
Beesy	*Age 3*
Annie	*Age 1*

I don't know how my parents met. I imagine they would have met in a pub or in the town somewhere, got to really like each other.

In the late 1920's Beazie married Larry McCarthy. He was from Cork. Everyone called him Mac. The Noones (I think it was all of them rather than just Beazie and Mac) bought another house, two along, in John's Row. After that, Granny, Annie and Katie lived in the original house and Beazie and Mac McCarthy lived in the new house. The Cusacks lived in the house between.

Beazie and Mac had two children, a boy (Larry) and a girl (Philomena). They also had one more girl who they called 'Marina', but Marina died very young. My sister, Kit, called her girl 'Marina' after the cousin Marina that died. Marina was three years old and Kit and I saw her lying on her death bed with a ring of flowers around her. Aunt Beazie put her on the double bed.

Granny Noone was a nice lady. She was very elegant and always wore black lace and fitted clothes. She wore her hair in a grey bun at the back of her head. She liked Mammy.

Dad's three sisters, Annie, Katie and Beazie, despised Mammy. They made it clear to me as I was growing up that they believed their Jim had married beneath him. I do not know if it was because Mammy was a 'servant girl', or whether it was known that she had been born in a Workhouse to a mother who had had two illegitimate children. Certainly, the Noones were not of much higher standing than Mammy, who looked after and was loved and trusted by several wealthy Westport families. Also certainly, my Nan didn't help matters. She didn't care what people thought. She was poor but not ashamed at all. She wore a shawl and old clothes and boots.

My greatest regret is that I do not have a photograph of Nan. In 1949 when I was in London, I visited my Aunt Mamie. She brought out a photo of Nan outside St Murdachs Cathedral having a wee with her legs spread apart. You'd never think that she was piddling and having her photo taken at the same time. I asked *"Can I have it?" "Oh, God no"*. .... Mamie said *"Oh no, you can't have it, it's all I've got of my Mother. I couldn't give it to you"*. I understood completely and said *"Okay, never mind"*. I would love to have a photo of my Nan. Over the years I have made many attempts to locate that photo but I have not been able to.

I was born in December 1932, so I must have been conceived around March 1932. James and Margaret Noone got married at St Mary's Church in Westport on the 14th of April 1932. Their marriage certificate shows Mammy gave her father's name as 'Michael Barrett' which was, of course, not true (that was her grandfather's name). I feel sorry for her that she felt she had to lie.

Granny Noone (born Mary Heraty), 1951

I always thought my parents were obliged to get married quickly when they discovered Mammy was pregnant with me. One reason I thought this is because my name was left off a certificate of marriage (i.e. not the actual marriage certificate) which my parents obtained on the 18th of June 1940. On the back of the certificate, the Registrar of Births, Deaths and Marriages (P. O'Grady) wrote;

The children of these parents were born on the following dates:-

Kitty Philomena	*4th October 1934*
Patrick Laurence	*14th August 1936*
James Christopher	*14th November 1937*
Margaret Anne	*15th September 1939*

My youngest brother Tom is not listed because he wasn't born until 1942, but the interesting thing is that I am not named in the list. That always caused me to wonder if Mammy and Dad were trying to hide my birth. I don't actually know for sure if I was ever baptised. Maybe the Registry only had a record of the children born in Westport.

This certificate describes Dad as the son of 'Thomas Noone and Mary Heraty' but it describes Mammy as the 'daughter of Margaret Barrett'. This indicates that P.O'Grady was not fooled by the actual marriage certificate. He knew Mammy did not have a known father.

The Registrar's Certificate describes Mammy as 'of the Mall, Westport'. That address reflects the fact that Mammy was working and living at the O'Malley's house at that time. Mammy left the O'Malley's house on the morning of her wedding. Mammy had no wedding ring so Mrs O'Malley bought her one. That shows the regard the O'Malleys had for Mammy.

I now see that their wedding was 8½ months before my birth so, while it is possible that they married as soon

Katie Noone with Paulie Lampert, 1978

Sometime that evening, Uncle Tom probably thought that

as Mammy missed her period, it is also possible that they did not conceive me or know about me until after they got married. The timing of my birth shouldn't have caused any fuss in the town. I mean, lots of children are born at 8½ months; it's not as if I was born three months out of wedlock or something like that.

I was not born in Westport. I was born in Ballina. I think Mammy and Dad went to Ballina to have me so Nan could support Mammy. I'm sure another factor was that the Noones (Annie, Katie, Beazie) were hostile. I don't think my parents would have stayed long in Ballina because Dad would not have been able to earn money there. Now that I think about it, it is possible that Mammy went to Ballina on her own to have me, just to be close to Nan.

I was born in the District Hospital of Ballina. I was named Mary Christina Noone. In my birth certificate, my Dad's name was given wrongly as 'James Noonan from Ballina' when we know he was James Noone from Westport. Mammy's name was given as 'Margaret Noonan (formerly Barrett)'. My Dad's occupation was given as 'Mendicant' which is a gypsy or a traveller or an odd job man, which he wasn't. He was a shoemaker.

As I said, I always thought my parents deliberately gave wrong information to disguise my birth but now that I realise they got married in Westport, all quite openly, I am beginning to wonder whether the details on the documents are just simple mistakes. All the Noones knew Mammy was pregnant so there was no point in hiding my birth.

After Mammy had me, she returned to Westport and

resumed working for the O'Malley's. I know this because when I went back to Ireland for the first time, in 1974, I met Nan O'Malley who was one of the O'Malley children that Mammy looked after. Nan O'Malley told me Mammy worked for them for quite a long time after I was born. She remembered Mammy cleaning their shoes on a Saturday night for church in the morning. She said they just loved her; she was a second mother to them. Yes, that's what I remember.

CHAPTER TWO

1932-1940
Living At Home

My early years, from what I can remember, were happy.

When Mammy and Dad brought me home from Ballina they were living in a house, just before you go onto the railway. The Fannons owned it after we did. In 1936 when I was nearly four, we left that house and moved across the road to a place which had a garret. You could climb up into this loft and sleep. It had a sloped ceiling. With the help of Google maps I have seen this house. It is the last house on the left down what is now known as Monument Street, off High Street.

The reason I remember this house with the loft is because one night Mammy and Dad decided to go out (probably down to the pub, I can't remember). They asked Dad's brother, Tom, to sit with me and (probably) my younger sister Kit (who would have been a baby). They said *"Look after her and we'll be back soon"*.

he should be down at the pub having a drink as well. So, he got a candle and he lit it and he put it in my hand and he put me sitting at the fireplace on the hob and I'm sitting there with the candle. It was burning down and I was just sitting there. He'd gone down to the pub and of course Mammy and Dad came home and I was still sitting there in the dark with the candle.

You know there were no lights. We didn't have any electricity. So *"What's happened here? Did Uncle Tom go out?"* and I said I didn't know much about where he went or anything. And they were talking to each other. I remember that very vividly like it was yesterday, and sitting there with this candle and wondering what was going to happen. I'm sure Uncle Tom would have heard about it later.

At some point, my parents bought the house in High Street where I grew up. I don't know how they afforded it. Probably paid it off. It was demolished and replaced in the 1990s. It is the last house before High Street veers into Monument Street. The earliest I can recollect about this house is when I was about five and it was New Year's Day. We didn't have a bathroom, we had a great big basin. Dad had the basin on a pedestal and was washing himself down. He said *"I'll have to be careful what I do when I throw this water out because whatever you do on New Year's Day, then you do it the whole year round"*. I'll always remember that and he had this soap and was really giving himself a good old wash. And so it must be the 1st of January, 1937. I had only just turned four in the December. So they had bought the house before then.

We had come through the Depression and no one thought

about a Second World War, least of all me in 1938 aged five. I had been going to school since I was three years old, same as all other kids in Ireland at that time. Mammy and Dad were making a home and, by 1938, there were four children. There was me about to turn six in the December; Kit who would turn four years in the October; Larry who would turn two in the August and James who would turn one in November 1938.

One of my earliest memories is getting up Christmas morning in 1938. Kit and I had a small doll each and Larry and James, two trucks, and they were wheeling them all over the bedroom floor.

Mammy never, ever, lost her temper with us although I will say this, I must have done something one day that she wasn't very happy about because I remember I argued with her a bit and I ran out the front door, and I ran down High Street and she ran down after me and I ran around the clock and she ran around the clock after me and on the way up she belted me and when we got up High Street, I was still crying and she must have felt terrible about it because she had an egg in the cupboard and she boiled the egg and made me sit down on a chair and put a little table in front of me to try to make up for it. I would have been about four or five; I wouldn't be any more than that, when that happened.

At this time, Dad worked on the roads, wearing an overcoat and a cap. Dad was on the steamroller and the crusher. I know of pavements that Dad actually worked on at the Quay in Westport. I even remember bringing Dad his lunch, running all the way. Two pieces of bread with a piece

High St, Westport

of steak and a flask of tea. Dad smoked Woodbines from the age of 14 and he would be having a smoke in the shed or tent. The pay for roadworks was £1.55 a week, but it was better than being on the dole, which happened in between jobs. When Dad had no work, he got fed up and queued every Wednesday morning for the dole. I think it was only five shillings so Dad would then take shoes in to mend to supplement his dole money. Mammy would scrub floors and do washing and clean houses. She would often return home with food and I have known her to carry a bag of potatoes on her back and walk quite a way home.

Dad went into the Free State Army in about 1939 because there was not enough work on the roads. The Irish Republic was neutral during the Second World War so Dad's Army service was all in Ireland. He was based on The Curragh, in County Kildare which is in the east of Ireland, near County Dublin.

Mammy worked for people who had their own businesses, not just the O'Malley family who lived on the Mall, but also the Goldens who lived on Bridge Street and they owned a toy shop, and the Shanleys who owned a clothes shop. Mammy did mostly housework and minded children.

Mammy had a gentle voice and because I was the first born and she had five more after me, I was the one who helped her a lot, if there was anything to be done. In fact, I grew up before my time.

I could set the fire (I knew where the coal was under the stairs) and I knew the turf; you put the kindling in first and put the little sods of turf around them. There were three fireplaces in the house, one in the kitchen and two upstairs, where we all slept. We were four in a bed. There was me and Kit at the top, and Larry and James at the bottom. When Margo came along, she had a little crib. But usually us four slept together. I don't remember ever in my life getting into a pair of pyjamas or anything like that. We took our jumper off and our skirt or whatever, and then went into bed in our vest and pants.

One of the upstairs fireplaces was in a room which nobody ever used. It was a lovely big room and the only thing I can

Our house in High Street (1976)
My nephew, Terry (Kit's son), standing outside

think about is that, way in the distance, I could see an old record player and a great big horn coming out of it. And that was always there; anytime you went into that room, that's the first thing you'd see and nothing else. There were no couches or carpets anywhere. I mean, we all slept in the one bed. I think that we were so poor that they just couldn't get us beds. Looking back on my life, why would we all be in one bed if they could afford a room nobody ever used?

Our bedroom looked onto High Street. Us kids' bed was right beside the window (the top, right window in the photograph). Mammy and Dad's bed was next to us and then (I can see it like it was yesterday) there was this great big, like a half circle, coming out and it had brown wallpaper or something like that on it and that's where we could keep, I don't know, whatever Mammy wanted for us kids at night like cough mixture or ointment, that's where that was. It was a big room.

There was a third room upstairs at the back and it was a very tiny room. It had a little window. On Sunday morning after Mass, Dad would take Kit and me up the road. Mammy would stay home with Larry and James and cook the usual Sunday dinner of bacon and cabbage. Dad would take us to where he played *"bullets"* (that's where you'd fling a heavy ball way into the distance and all the men used to do that). But when Dad finished that, he'd come back for us and he used to take me and Kit and we'd walk right past our Granny's place (I don't remember ever stopping there) and we'd go right up and he'd say *"This is where I play bullets"*, that's what he called it.

Players Please
THOMAS MORAN
LIZ 69

When we'd get home Mammy would have cooked bacon and cabbage, and not only that, she would have made trifle. There were no fridges but because the weather was always cool, Mammy gave me the trifle and I'd walk upstairs into that little room and I'd put it out onto the ledge and by the time we had our dinner, the trifle would be set and then she'd have a tin of reduced cream to have with it.

Mammy cooked on an open fire. There was no cooker or anything like that. Mammy had what she called an *"oven."* It was a round, cast iron pot and it had a big lid on it. Mammy would cook stews, cakes, bread and lovely rhubarb pies in there. The oven had a handle that could hang from the top. You had a hook that slid along an iron bar going from one side of the fire to the other and two hobs, where you could even sit in (I've done that lots of times, sit in the hob and you'd be nearer the fire). You'd just take the iron bar off, hook your oven on and leave it there. You'd know how long it took. And yeah, it was beautiful.

Oh, the rhubarb pie Mammy used to make. She would make a big turf fire and while she waited for that to be roaring, with lots of red coals, Mammy would make the pastry. She would cover the bottom of the oven, cut up the rhubarb and put that in, sprinkle sugar over it, put the rest of the pastry on top, put one or two holes in the top to let out the steam and when the pie was cooked, we would stand around and wait for it to cool and then we all got a piece. All the lovely sugar and syrup would be at the bottom of the oven. We'd all be on the floor with the oven and we'd be spooning it out. Mammy always had a bucket of water to

Opposite: Bridge St, Westport

wash the oven, she'd just put the water in there. If it was too sticky she'd boil a kettle of water and put it in, let it steep and then just get a scrubbing brush and scrub it.

Mammy would use a cast iron pan to fry the steak in for Dad (because we never got any of that). I used to get the steak from the O'Malleys. Mammy used to say *"Go to Mrs O'Malley's today because today's the day the butcher comes and he delivers some meat there"*. They had a cold store out in this big back kitchen and it had a great big fireplace in it. They had an outside scullery, a place for washing up. Their sink was made of something like concrete and it was varnished over so that it didn't have the awful look of concrete and they had two taps over it. So the O'Malleys had running water and I guess the Kennys and Mr and Mrs Plunket would have - all those people Mammy used to work for. They had everything, Mammy said, *"So, she'll know that you're there and Mrs O'Malley will give you a couple of bits of steak and that's for your Dad"*. I'd only have to appear there and I wouldn't have to say anything. She would give me two pieces of steak.

I remember Dad getting up in the morning when he was working on the roads. In Ireland we had four seasons in one day and I remember Dad putting a big old overcoat on him and a cap and Mammy making his lunch some mornings. Other days I used to come home for lunch. I would have run from the town school in Altamount Street. This school was near and inside the Convent gates. I'd run all the way up High Street, and Mammy would be frying a little bit of steak and putting it in a bit of bread and I'd run over to the Quay because they were putting in the paths and he'd be sitting in an old shed with the other men, waiting for his lunch, and I'd just give it to him and then I'd run all the way back home. If I had time, I'd have a bit of bread and jam and if I didn't have time, I'd run straight back to school.

We had a wooden table and every Saturday morning it would be taken out onto the street (Mammy started doing it, but then it was my job) to scrub it, scrub it and then throw all the water over. We'd go over to the pump and get buckets of water, throw it over. The same with the chairs and they'd come up like new. The pump is still there, directly opposite our house. To this very day.

Mammy loved the table to be clean. We didn't have anything so that's probably something that she enjoyed doing. I mean, we had flagstones on the floor, great big crooked flagstones. When James was little, we had a tea chest and she'd take all that paper off the tea chest but one day, there was a little bit of tinsel hanging out and James was jumping up and down in the tea chest and he caught his diddle in it. That was terrible.

Mammy cooked the spuds on the open fire. On a Sunday, she'd put a big piece of bacon on first and boil that and then she'd put the cabbage in with the bacon and the bacon water, and then she'd get another iron pot and put all the potatoes in and then boil them.

If you went up to Granny's, it would be the same thing. Mammy didn't mind us going to see Granny.

You'd see Aunt Katie with an iron fry pan and she'd have made a lovely Irish soda bread and she put the cross on it and she'd put the pan over really hot coals and then she'd put the bread in on top of there to cook. And she sat there (and it was a tiring thing, I used to see her doing it) and every

My granddaughter Madeline by the pump 2019.
People are looking in the window of
the house that replaced ours.

now and then she'd flip it over. When it was done she'd take it off there and give us a bit of it. It was lovely. You could smell it and it was lovely to have a bit of that bread. The fry pan would rest on the hot coals.

The fireplace in the postcard on the next page is exactly

like ours and this is exactly how Mammy baked Irish bread, made stews and boiled the kettle, only Mammy didn't wear a shawl. The oven is the big black pot on the right.

After school most days I would pick brambles in the woods so Mammy could light the fire in the morning. Then I'd go to Burkes Garage down on Bridge Street and knock on the kitchen door and ask politely *"Is there anything left over after your dinner?"* The maid would put the leftover food in newspaper and I would go home happy we would have something to eat. Their oven was heated by coal or turf, but mostly by coal. There was a side where you could put the coal. Nobody who I knew of in Westport in the 1930s, was cooking with electricity or anything like that.

We had two or three kerosene lamps hanging on the wall so we could see our way around. If you were going up to bed, you brought the small lamp up with you. They were called *"Sacred Heart Lamps"* – they were about four or five inches high. They had a little bubble that you put the kerosene in and a tiny little wick and it gave you enough light to get into bed.

Mammy called our toilet *"the garden shed"*. It was a shed in our garden and it was full of straw. We'd go out there and do number 1s or number 2s and we would lay straw on top. It was turned over now and then. Then we'd get some more straw. Most houses in Westport were in that situation at that time. All the ones on High Street would have been; they'd have no running water, they'd have no sink or anything like that. This was around 1939.

In the more wealthy houses, they would usually use a

Postcard depicting cooking on the hearth

bucket in the house. Some people, like the Kenny's, they had two toilets. They had one in their house and they had one outside and it flushed. I remember flushing the toilet, looking down and thinking *"There's going to be water everywhere"*. So flush toilets were available to those who could afford them.

My Dad hung all the wallpaper in our house. What I remember mostly about the wallpaper is that at the very top there was about four inches of a lining going the whole way around, like a *"finishing off"* thing. I think it is called a 'frieze'. They'd bring the wallpaper up so far and then they'd have a lining going all the way around. I think that only the little kitchen had wallpaper and as you go up the stairs, that had a nice sort of floral wallpaper.

We had two rooms off the kitchen. Sometimes we let one of the rooms for five shillings a week, mostly to a Mary Salmon, a small woman, hair severely combed back. She wore long dresses, white aprons, high buttoned black boots which were always clean. Mary Salmon used to boil her water to make tea in a small tin. We had an open fireplace. Often, Larry (my brother) who would only have been about four to five years at the time, would occasionally throw soot in the tin, but with the tin being tarnished on the inside and with Mary Salmon being a little short-sighted, the tea was tossed into the boiling water and, with a cloth, Mary would take the tin to her room and drink it.

I think in Mary Salmon's room, her walls were probably white-washed. And also where my Dad mended the shoes. The kitchen, like I say, was only very little but I remember just as you went upstairs, we had about that much space where we hung pictures and then the rest of it carried on from there, up the stairs. As far as I can remember, in our bedroom where we all slept, it probably was white-washed.

There was a window at the top of the stairs and then you'd turn around left and that's where our bedroom was. The window at the top of the stairs looked out onto our garden at the back of the house. It threw some light onto the staircase.

We had curtains in the kitchen (we only had a little window in the kitchen that looked out over onto the pump on High Street) and Mammy had a little lace curtain in there. Nothing that kept the heat in or the cold out. If you are looking at the house, this little window is on the right of the front door. And we had no form of heating. The fire would be lit and that was it. The rooms were freezing so we were often cold at night. But I mean, they did the best they could for us.

When we did get a bath..... I was just thinking the other day (God rest Mammy's soul) ... she was a very clean woman and she loved everything lovely and clean. She loved to get dressed up when she could. I often wonder (because we never had any shower, we only had a little bath) and I wondered how she got on. I often think to myself (well, not often, but sometimes it comes into my mind) ... I remember Dad, he had a great big basin and when he'd come home from the Army he'd bring Lifebuoy soap home and we thought that was great. It had a horrible smell but to us (because we were used to Sunlight) it was special. Sunlight soap is great for washing your hair; it brings all the lights up. Mind you, it's not good for your scalp I suppose, but your hair looks good.

Once when Dad was mending shoes, I decided to play with my dolls' set of cups and saucers. They were too high up on the shelves so I asked Dad to get them for me. He didn't seem to hear, but I kept on and on. He got up, went to the cupboard, said *"Do you want these cups and saucers?"* I said *"yes"*. He threw all of them on the floor, smashed all except one, then walked back and continued to mend the shoes. I suppose I shouldn't have kept on, but then I was only a child.

I've mentioned Dad's three sisters, Katie, Annie and Beazie. Dad also had two brothers, Tom and Martin, both older than Dad.

Uncle Tom lived just across the road from our place, in High Street, and he was married to Mary and they had five children – Paddy, Tommy, Mary, Lil and Jim and we knew all our cousins because they were just living across the road.

Tom was in the Army but what he did as a job, I don't know. Maybe he worked on the roads with Dad because at that time, working on the roads was about all people could do. They never ended up being doctors or lawyers or anything like that.

Mary died in 1940, with heart disease. I remember the day she died because I went into Mrs Kitrick's and I said that Aunt Mary had died and she put me sitting out on the pavement with a cushion underneath me and gave me a bit of bread and sugar (there might have been a bit of butter or that, but it was very scarce) but I remember the sugar being there and I was sitting there. Later on in the day, I went up to the Noones (my Aunts Annie, Beazie, Katie and Granny) and I just mentioned that Aunt Mary had died and Aunt Anne said to me *"Yes, we know. It's a pity it's not that cat-of-a-Mother of yours that died"* and so I came down and I told my Mammy but she, like always, said to me *"Don't worry about it; it's nothing"*. She never commented on it, never said anything. I remember her sometimes saying *"Every dog has his day."*

When Aunt Mary died, Uncle Tom was wondering what was going to happen to the five children, but at that time no one seemed to be interested in having them and he kept the kids together for maybe six months, it could be longer. But one day the gypsies (like tinkers) came in to Westport and they had all their caravans coming down the road and the kids saw him just walk out of his house, got on a caravan, and no one ever heard from him again.

Aunt Beazie took Paddy. He would have been about 20

but he was wetting the bed. How I know that was (I was only about seven) I remember going up one day to Aunt Beazie's house and I felt really sorry for Paddy because he walked out of the room as she was telling him off for peeing in the bed. To me, he looked quite grown-up. But, poor soul, he was only young. 20 was young. Anyway, he stayed there for quite a while. I'm not saying she was awful to him; it's just that, that's what happened.

Tommy, I think the McBrides took him in and they lived on Peter Street. I don't know much about Tommy; I didn't see an awful lot of him. Bridget McGee (who lived on High Street) was an Aunt of Aunt Mary. She took Mary. She got Mary a job at the Smiths who had a nice house on Mill Street, looking after the children and doing odd jobs there, cleaning and that.

Lil, nobody wanted her. Nobody wanted Lil at all. We took her in for a little while and she was just finishing school at 14, because she wasn't that clever. I remember the last day of her school, she came home with her books. I remember sitting down and she was reading the stories out of her reading book. I asked her if I could have it and she gave it to me. So, that was lovely and knowing Mammy, she would have said *"Stay here because there's no place else. I could put you up a bed or a mattress on the floor"* or whatever, I don't know. But I know that she was with us after she finished school, for a while. I know that Lil ended up with nowhere to live. Police picked her up and put her in the orphanage. Lil escaped by scaling the Convent gates and ran to Mrs Reilly's house. Mrs Reilly put her in the window box when the police came to look for her.

Tom and Mary Noone

Jim, the youngest, was about 12. On High Street, just down from Bridget McGee where Mary went, there was the Walshes - Mr and Mrs Walsh, and they couldn't get enough of this little fellow. They took him in, reared him, sent him to school, bought him all his clothes, everything. Eventually, he went into the Army. What I remember about Jim, as a young person, after his Mother died, Mammy would pay him and give him a meal for doing jobs like when the coal man came, he'd take the coal and he'd put it all under the stairs for her and he'd go up into the woods and he'd chop some trees down for kindling wood for the fire. To me, he always had like an Army coat on, a big Army coat. So, Mammy was really good to him; did what she could. He could come in and out to our place.

In Aughavale Cemetery, just inside the gate on the left, there is a grave of Baby Noone. That is Mary Noone. She was known as Baby Noone.

I don't think the Noones would have been embarrassed that Tom had gone off with the gypsies. I think they were happy when he left because that just left the girls there with Gran and they could still hold their heads up high because, as far as everyone knew, Tom had left Westport to find work.

We saw quite a bit of Dad's brother, Martin, when we were growing up. To my knowledge, he lived in Castlebar with his wife and kids but strangely he never brought his wife and kids (our auntie and cousins) to Westport so I never met any of them. Martin was always in Westport and he'd come along and he'd have a meal with us or maybe Dad and him would go down to The West pub and have a drink. Yeah, I liked Uncle Martin a lot; I had a lot of time for him. To me, he was someone that used to come in and we always had good feelings. He worked on the roads. I saw a lot of Uncle Martin when I was small. He used to sing *"The Flowers of Sweet Strabane"*. I never heard the Noones saying a bad word about Martin.

Once a month all the farmers from the surrounding areas (Caillte Mách (which means *"from the woods"*)), would walk all their cattle into town especially up Mill Street and onto the Fair Green. (I'm not talking here about the town of Kiltamagh which is on the other side of Castlebar.)That's where we used to walk to school and there would be cow shit everywhere and we'd have to walk through it. We would stand and watch the farmers doing deals. They'd be all clapping their hands to say *"Right! Is that all for them?"* They'd spit on their hands when a deal went through and shake on it.

There were other regular markets. On Shop Street by the fountain, that's where the markets were held, say, every three months. They'd come up from Ballinrobe, and down from Castlebar and Ballina, the towns around Westport. They'd set up their little stalls and they'd put out all their wares. The men who were coming down from Ballina would have collected stuff and tried to sell it in the Square in Ballina. If they had stuff left over they would catch a bus down to Westport and try and sell it. One of the Ballina men knew my Nan. When he came to Westport, Mammy would have collected things given to her by the Shanleys (sometimes there were new shoes, maybe vests and pants, maybe little tops and things like that) and she'd wait for that man to call when he had finished selling in the Shop Street market. If

Dad had mended any shoes they would go into the parcel Mammy would give to this man, and when he got back to Ballina he would give the parcel to my Nan.

The shoes Dad mended might have come from the Walsh's on Barrack Hill. There were about four girls in that family. I don't know how well-off they were but they could afford to say to Dad *"Jim, here's a pair of shoes. If there's someone who you think would need them"*. And then Dad would put soles and heels on them.

There was a cinema in Westport, in Shop Street. That's where my Dad used to go. I don't remember Mammy and Dad going out together, except that one time when they went to the pub and left me with Uncle Tom. My Dad loved cinema and he loved Fred Astaire and I think he thought he could dance like Fred Astaire. There was a dance hall in Westport, also in Shop Street, across the road from Gibbonses. This was the shop where you could buy all sorts of things and they pulled a cord and it shot the canister to the office upstairs, and it came back with the change and receipt.

Say you're walking up High Street, our house is the last street on the left before High Street diverts left into what is now called Monument Street. Well just up there, in Monument Street, was Tom Carroll who was a great friend of Dad's and so we'd go up there, or to Mr and Mrs Flynn's who lived beside Tom's. Aunt Katie used to sing a song *"There's hair on my belly, there's hair on my chin, there's hair on the balls of old Antony Flynn"*. And you know, we didn't know what balls were or anything like that. And we'd all laugh,

Larry McCarthy, Philly McCarthy, Beazie McCarthy (I don't know if Granny even picked it up) but that was Kate. She'd laugh and laugh and laugh. And us kids would look at each other. So the Flynns were up there and they were really nice.

While I remember, two brothers lived on the hill, Paddy and Michael O'Malley. They kept hens. An egg cost a penny. It was my job to get an egg when Mammy needed one. One day, when I was seven, I had gone twice and bought an egg and on the third time, Michael O'Malley said to me *"Does your Mother think my hens have two arse holes?'* When I repeated it to Mammy, she said *"Wait until I see Mick O'Malley; I'll give him a piece of my mind'*. Paddy was tall and they used to call him *Corncrake* which is a bird.

Going back a bit to when I was about five, every evening at 7.00pm Rosary was said in St Mary's Church. Michael O'Malley always went. He was a little man, bent over and he passed our door on his way. I used to stand at my door and as Mick went past, I'd join him and walk down High Street with him and along Bridge Street to the church; then Mick would take me home. I remember I wore a brown hat as those days, a woman had to cover her head going into a church. About this time, I had an ear ache. Michael O'Malley said he had a cure. Mammy said she would try anything. He told Mammy to light a big turf fire and peel an onion. She put the tongs in the fire until they were red hot. Michael O'Malley took the tongs out of the fire and picked up the onion in them and put it close to my ear, said something like a ritual and he told me my earache would go and it did. It was very painful because the tongs were hot and very close to my ear. I was very upset.

Around this time, all of us children didn't look too good, pale and listless. Mammy thought we could have worms. There is a weed that you pick and boil, and the contents you swallow. Well, we had to drink this remedy. I don't think Mammy was prepared for what was to come. We had tapeworms. When we went to the toilet, Mammy would stand there with the tongs and had to pull the worms out of us. They were so long; somebody said it was the water we drank.

When I think about Mammy, she loved going out. She worked for Shanleys of course, and they were very good to her. They gave her some lovely clothes. Mammy loved to get dressed up and I remember them giving her a mustard coat. It had lapels, like a military coat, and they gave her a lovely brown hat and I can see her like it was yesterday and she was standing in the kitchen (and I don't know where Mammy and Dad were going), but they walked out the door and she just looked beautiful; lovely black hair, Mammy had jet black hair. She never got her hair done, never wore make-up. I never, ever saw her with a bit of lipstick on, never had a thing on her face – really nice skin, you know. And really loveable.

Dad played the melodeon. We used to love it because it was up on a top shelf and when we were all sitting around, he'd take it down and play it; he was a good player, like all Irish people, I mean they're just into music, you know. And we loved that and it always sat up on top of this lovely buffet hutch that he had made. He even made the two doors on the side. They had to have latches – he made them all, everything. You've got to give him that.

Dad did all the gardening, he put all the potatoes in every year, the scallions and strawberries. Dad would go out there and he'd turn all the soil over and then he'd put in these King Edward potatoes and they were absolutely gorgeous. I mean, these potatoes today are nice and I like them and all that, but oh... in the old days when you peeled the King Edwards, all the flour was underneath and they'd mash so easy, that's what they were called, anyway. The Irish love mashed potatoes with spring onions, and salted butter which we got from a lady up the road who used to make it. And then in another plot he'd have a row of spring onions (we used to call them *scallions*), another row was taken up with strawberries. He wasn't a gardener but somehow or other, in between making the shoes and all that, he'd find time to go out in the garden. We were never short of blackcurrants. You could make jam out of them if you wanted, but they were very small berries and we used to eat them.

And also our next door neighbours, the Giblins, had lovely bushes of very nice smelling roses and their roses used to come into our garden, so when no one was looking, we'd pick the roses and we'd have logan berries as well.

Our great, big, long garden had two spring wells. One was ours, it was on our section, and the other one was on the other side. We would get the water up with a bucket. It was an old thing, you had to really drag it up. But it wasn't that far down, you could see the magnificent clean water. We used to look down into it and we'd obviously see ourselves. But not at any time, I never ever remember either Mammy or Dad saying *"Be careful, don't fall in the well"*. We had no running water, so the spring water was a great help, although we did draw buckets of water from the pump opposite our house.

As you looked at our house, on the left hand side was the O'Malleys. There were at least three different O'Malley families that I knew of in Westport. These O'Malleys, our neighbours, had a cow. The cow would be kept in their back paddock at night and in the morning Mr O'Malley would bring the cow through the house and up to the paddocks where I used to get the butter from Mrs Mohan. Less than a mile up the road. At night time, Mr O'Malley would bring the cow back home and milk it. They had a small grocery shop at the front of their house where they also sold the milk from the cow.

I have said that Dad was a really good shoemaker. I don't imagine he had an apprenticeship. I think maybe he just worked with someone at the time and that's how he learned his trade. There were shoe shops, but if someone couldn't get shoes that they wanted (made purely from leather) they would go to a shoemaker. Kit spent lots of time with Dad in the little room but I also know how it goes because I sometimes used to go down and watch him work. He had the hemp and the thread. He used to pull this hemp along the thread and make the thread so tight and whatever he put on it (the hemp, obviously) and then he had an awl. I knew how he cut the sole out of these shoes and then just to put it onto the main shoe and then, what he'd do is, he'd bore the holes with this awl and then he'd thread this hemp thread all the way through until he had the whole lot done. It was just great to see. Dad mainly mended shoes rather than made them.

Dad had a dog called Ivy and he also had a ferret and the ferret was always in the cage and I never saw the ferret come out of the cage (and I don't know what Dad fed him on because we were never there when it was fed, but obviously it was fed on something). Every Sunday Dad used to take Ivy, and the ferret in a cage, and he'd walk up High Street, right up onto a road up there. If you kept on going, it was where I used to get the butter for the potatoes. So, I knew where they were going and sometimes he'd take Georgie Hastings with him.

I liked Georgie Hastings and I got Mammy to dress me up one day in a lovely dress that somebody had given her and she said *"Why is that?"* and I said *"Because I want to stand outside the door and when Georgie Hastings goes past, he'll see me"* and she said *"Oh okay then"*. So one day when he went past, she called him and he came in. He was a grown man but I had a crush on him.

But nearly every Sunday Georgie Hastings used to come to our place and Dad and him used to go way into the woods and they'd come home with two or three rabbits. That was always great because when they came home with rabbits, they would skin them and then Mammy would boil them and we would have rabbit stew and that would last us just about all the week. One night they came home and we were all sitting at the fire and I said to Georgie *"Can I come and please sit on your lap?"* and he'd say *"Yeah, yeah course you can"* and made a real fuss of me. My first crush, you know.

The ferret would go down into the hole, drive the rabbit out and the dog would get him and kill him. That's how that was done. The ferret was down in a little room and he had a nice little place on his own and we used to go down there and we peered through and we always used to look at his eyes and that. But he was fat and he was happy, he had nice bedding underneath him and things like that and I'm sure that Dad would have taken him out of the cage. He must have treasured the ferret because without the ferret there'd be no rabbits.

A lot of people in the town used ferrets and dogs to catch rabbits. Just about all the people that I knew that were of our kind and had not an awful lot of money, lived on rabbits.

Ivy was a greyhound. Then we had Fido and he was like a West-Highland Terrier. They never took him hunting. He was left home with us. He'd say *"Come on Ivy"* and Ivy would be only too happy to go with Dad. So there were one or two dogs in the house when I was growing up. Quite a few people owned dogs. Whatever they had, they always made sure that, even if it was just like Oxo and bread or whatever they could, they fed the dogs with that; they never went hungry.

Mrs Gannon (not Patricia Gannon) lived across the road from us by the water pump. She was a dressmaker. Mammy got Mrs Gannon to make two dresses for Kit and I. Mine was white with green stripes and Kit's was white with red stripes.

Patricia Gannon was Mammy's best friend. I named my first daughter Margaret, after Mammy, and I named my second daughter Patricia, after Patricia Gannon. Before she got married, Patricia was a McGreevy. Mammy worked for the McGreevys and that's how she became good friends with Patricia. On a Sunday morning Patricia and her mother and father used to serve in the shop ('McGreevy's'). They sold everything - ice-cream, groceries, toys, pots and pans. Some Sundays Patricia used to serve on her own while her Mum and Dad attended early Mass. Mammy knew what Sundays Patricia was there on her own. Then I got up early, went to 7.00am Mass. Mammy would give me a penny just in case Patricia wasn't there. After Mass, I would go across the road to the shop, have the one penny ready if Mr McGreevy came to serve me and I'd ask for a penny ice-cream, but if Patricia was there, I would wait my turn then Patricia would make a parcel up of sausages, black pudding and bacon and hand it to me. I would also have my penny so Mammy could buy an egg later. When I got home, Daddy would be in bed. Mammy would look delighted with the parcel and we would all eat well.

There was Swift's shop where the two sisters used to sell cigarettes. Swifts shop was on Shop Street and wasn't far from the midwife with the Alsatian dog. When you went in to Swifts, the two big fat sisters used to be behind the counter; one would be measuring out maybe a bit of sugar or a bit of tea. If you had four pennies, well you'd get four pennies' worth of tea. They would sell most things. Oil, you know like for lamps and things like that. They'd let you fill your own lamp, whatever you had that you had the oil in. Tommy Giblin would give me two pennies. One penny for two cigarettes and one penny for me. Tommy Giblin would come in and he'd say *"I'll give you a wing"* (a "wing" was a penny) *"You keep a wing for yourself and get me two cigarettes"*, so I'd run down the street for them.

There was a very old lady who used to sell dillisk (seaweed) at the bottom of High Street. I never, ever, saw her stand up. Whenever I went past, she was always sitting on a chair with a great big sack and I'm sure that whoever put the dillisk in there would have really pushed it right down because she'd sit there all day. You could have a penny, tuppence-worth, threepence-worth, whatever you wanted. But even a penny's-worth would last you all day. It was like people chewing tobacco, it's like that; it's very, very chewy and very salty. You'd swallow it and you'd be very thirsty.

In Ballina they used to collect a seaweed that had little bubbles on it; it was called Carageen Moss. They used to boil it up and then strain it and then you'd get like a milk substance out of it. A mill was put up at the end of Ardnaree in Ballina where they used to make the Carageen Moss.

Outside the Bank of Ireland on the Mall there was a bay hedge. Mammy would take a few leaves and put them in the stew or whatever dish she was making. To this day, I have a bay tree in memory of Mammy. Most days I touch the leaves and say *"Wherever you are I hope you are happy."*

Every now and again there would be jumble sales. People would give clothes that had been worn and for sixpence you could get a nice dress. On one of the occasions Mammy bought me two dresses. One was brown with tiny flowers, but I loved the other one. It was blue with flowers. When I got home I asked Mammy if I could wear one of my dresses and I picked the blue one.

So, all the kids off High Street, we all went up to play on the railway tracks. You'd hear the toot of the old train and you knew not to be on the tracks. There was a big sort of a slope and so you'd all go down there until the train went past and then you'd be all up on the track again. This train would be going between Westport and Dublin. This day in particular they said *"Let's play diving down the slope"* and I was all in favour of that. We did it numerous times and the grass was wet and I never ever looked at my dress, I just thought this was lovely and I looked good (which was important). Anyway, on the way home I looked down at my dress and then I thought *"Oh my God!"* All the flowers that Mammy probably thought were printed fast, they all had dissolved. In fact, it just looked like a dirty white dress because all of the flowers had gone.

Anyway, I thought *"Oh, what am I going to do? I never want to wear this dress again"* so I came down and Mammy said *"Where have you been?"* and I said *"I've been up on the railway track"* and she said *"I can see that. Have you been tumbling down?"* and I said *"Yeah, I have"* and she wasn't very happy at all. She said *"Do you know how long it took me to get sixpence to buy that dress?"* I felt terrible but I still didn't realise how much sixpence was worth.

Hitler declared war on Poland on 31 August 1939, then England and France declared war on Germany on 3rd of September at 11.00am. I was six years old and would turn seven in December 1939.

Dad joined the Army before the war started. I think he joined because maybe at that time he wasn't earning much money. Dad was based at the Curragh, in County Kildare, which is close to Dublin. Once he joined the Army he was away a lot. He used to come home on leave and that's when we used to have to do all the things so that he could look, you know, very smart.

We had a great big basin and I remember Dad coming home from the Army. After he had washed with the Lifebuoy soap he would go down the street and go into The West pub, meet all his friends. To get him ready to go out, we used to sit on the stairs and he'd take his leather chappies from the bottom of his boot to the knee and he'd hand them to one of us. He'd give us his jacket and he had a thing that you'd put underneath the buttons and he'd give us the Brasso and we'd have to shine his buttons.

This was his Free State Army uniform and he had two cross guns on either side of his jacket which we had to polish for him as well. And he'd wash himself and then put on a nice shirt (although the shirt that he had didn't have a collar on it, 'cos the uniform used to come right up). His cap, he used to love his cap and his stick. And then he'd walk down High Street like if he'd come out of a hotel. People called him *"the dandy"*. He'd walk down High Street like he owned it, God rest his soul.

One month into the War, in September 1939, Nan came down from Ballina to look after us kids while Mammy had Margo. Dad was away in the Army. My first recollection about the War was that one night, when Mammy was due to

Me (5) and Kit (3) outside O'Malley's window, Mammy watching on.

give birth to Margo, she needed some water. Mammy was superstitious. As we were going to bed, Mammy said to Nan (she used to call her *"Mother"*) and she says, *"Mother, there's no water in the house"* so Nan said *"Oh, Mag we'll get it in the morning"* – Mammy said *"The spirits might want to drink"* (or something like that) *"... and I'd like for there to be water in the house"*. So, the next thing was, Nan said to me *"Okay then, let's go over to the pump and we'll get some water; it's just across the road"*. Nan took the bucket and opened the door. It was pitch dark and I said to Nan *"Why is it so dark?"* and she looked down at me and she said *"Because there's a war on"*.

Marina (Kit's daughter) and me
outside O'Malley's window in 2003

And I looked up at her and I didn't know what *"war"* was or anything like that. It was September 1939 so I wouldn't be seven until the December. The galvanised bucket would be put on the table and Mammy was always happy that a bucket of water was on the table; she knew that in the morning we would boil it up on the coals for a cup of tea or, for breakfast.

When Mammy was having Margo, Nan said to me *"It's time to get the midwife"*. I didn't know what a midwife was but I knew Mrs O'Malley was the midwife and I knew where she lived. I have mentioned she had the biggest Alsatian you ever did see and it used to lie on the footpath. When you'd go by it (even though you didn't know much about dogs), this Alsatian would be sitting there and that's where I used to go. I went down and I walked all the way back with Mrs O'Malley with her bag, up High Street, and she saw to Mammy. Margo was born on 15 September 1939. All the kids and me were upstairs in the bedroom with Mammy. She was walking up and down the room and sort of moaning. Mrs O'Malley kept telling me to turn away because I was the oldest and all that, poor Mammy, she was moaning and everything. We thought Nurse O'Malley was cutting her leg or something, we didn't know what was happening.

The next photograph was taken in our back garden while Dad was away in the Army. From left to right there is Kit, Mammy holding James, Larry and me. I would say this photo was taken in about 1940 when I was seven. I remember the day it was taken by Tony Fannon. The original of this photograph was held by my Dad and, after he died, Kit got copies of it for each of us. I treasure it.

One night we all woke up with a noise on the stairs. Dad was away in the Army. Mammy said *"Mother, could you go down and see what's happening because there's something happening on the landing?"* so Nan said *"Yes"* and I said *"I'll come with you"* so we walked out the door of that room where we all slept and we walked down the first few steps and we got onto the landing and we're standing on the landing, looking down, and there were two of the biggest rats I've ever seen. They were huge (they must have been water rats because they were so huge) and they were dragging our loaf of bread up the stairs that we were going to have for our breakfast. They were the size of cats. They were coming up towards us. Nan didn't know what to do. She said *"Well, they've got the loaf of bread. Mag, they've got the loaf of bread! We may as well let them have it and we'll see what we can do about the rats tomorrow"*. We closed the bedroom door and the next morning when we came down, the bread, what they'd not eaten of it, was on the stairs, but they were nowhere to be seen. So, they could have gone anywhere. I mean, they could have hid under the stairs as you go out to the garden and when we opened the door (because sometimes we had a latch on it and we'd leave that door open) they could have gone out there. We never caught them. I don't remember seeing any other rats ever.

I was going to the town school. This building is inside the Convent gate, on the left. Part of it is still standing today.

Apparently, I used to talk quite a bit in class and Sister Bernadette was always calling me out *"Maureen Noone, would you be quiet and not say so much?"* I would have been six then

Dad on the Curragh (with his hand on Gandhi's shoulder)

because you go into Sister Columba's when you're seven, so this was Sister Bernadette. Kit was just starting school and she was in Sister Dominic's class where all the dolls were up on the top shelf. There was no way that Kit was going to be happy. She was in the sandpit and she just wanted to go home. So, Sister Dominic came into Sister Bernadette's classroom and said *"Could I have Maureen Noone?"* and she said *"Oh yes, all right"*. She said *"Kitty is playing up a bit so we thought if Maureen was in there"*, so I went in there and I sat in the sandpit with her and that was okay.

It came to be half past 11 and really, I should have been at catechism, and I wasn't because I was in with Kit. And

Dad in his Free State Army uniform (on the left)

12 o'clock, then it was playtime. But as we were going into school at about half past 12 or quarter to one, Sister Bernadette came along the line and when she found me, she said *"You weren't at catechism"* and I said *"No"* and she took both my cheeks and she pinched them so hard that I had tears in my eyes. Then, a few days after that I was talking again in class and she put her hand way down into her pocket and she said *"Maureen Noone, you come up here"* so I went up to see her and she said *"I've got a safety pin and if you talk in class again, you know what I'm going to do?"* and I said *"No"* and she said *"I'm going to safety pin your lips together"*. I walked back to my seat. I was terrified. It made me shut up, that's for sure.

In those days nobody had a phone and very few people had a radio, so if anything happened – somebody died, say – a runner would be sent to tell the people who needed to know. Every family had a runner who would run from the top of High Street all the way down Bridge Street, Shop Street wherever and eventually go down there and they'd just go in and they'll say *"So and so has died"* or whatever had happened and that was the way news got around.

I went to Nan's place in Ballina three times before I was 9 (because I was 9 when Mammy got sick). I was aged 5, 6 and 7 or thereabouts. Nan lived at 60 Healy Terrace in Ardnaree. Healy Terrace runs on from Abbey Street where Nan was living in 1901 at the time of the Census. Nan's front door was on the right side of the house, not the left, in those days, and Nan used to sit at the window that was by that front door.

The first time I was five. This was when Dad was away

Kit, Mammy, James, Larry and me

in the Army, Mammy took all of us to Ballina on a holiday. It was great visiting Nan. She always had old dolls, balls and games for us. Nan's house was a council house that Nan would have rented initially when she was married to James McDermott. So, living in the house was Nan, James McDermott, Mamie and John McDermott and Uncle Billy.

If you continued down Healy Terrace you would reach Cealtra. It was a lovely little place; it had a river, stepping stones to get across the other side and lovely trees where we used to sit and have a picnic. Mammy let us go across the other side of the river on these step-stones. I mean, I wouldn't even let you guys do it but she was sitting there with her friends Alice Howley and Nanny Ginty. Remember Mammy was from Ballina, so she grew up with these friends. Nanny Ginty was the same age as Mammy but perhaps her name was Nancy and they called her *"Nanny"*. They'd sit there and they would have made us sandwiches and what-have-you and they let us go over to the other side. The water was there and we used to get over the other side and wave to them. They'd wait for us to come all the way back again and then we'd have our lunch.

Nanny Ginty and Alice Howley were great friends of Mammy. I remember one day Alice, Mammy, Kit and me (I don't know about any of the younger kids because I can't remember us having a pram with us) but we were coming up to Hannicks Public House, as you come up to go into Ardnaree. You left the main street where St Murdach's Cathedral is and you make your way up. Before you come to Ardnaree, Mammy and Alice Howley were talking, us kids were having a great time, skipping and all that and Alice Howley said *"Mag, I've swallowed a fly!"* Mammy said *"... don't keep your mouth open". "Oh, I think it's a midge; I don't know what it is but it's gone right down". "Don't worry about it; it will be all right"*. I imagine Nan would have looked after Larry, and James if he had been born then.

Nan's house was a much better quality house than our house in High Street, Westport. There was a bed downstairs where we all slept. The flush toilet was outside. Upstairs there were three bedrooms. They had plenty of room although the kitchen wasn't very big. There was an under-the-stairs where Nan used to keep the coal or the wood or whatever.

Tyrawley Park was a mile and a half from Healy Terrace. 19 Tyrawley Park was where Aunt Bidney (Mammy's sister) lived with her husband Joe Moyles. He was an odd-job man. Joe's aunt was Lizzie Ormsby. She lived around the road from number 19 – maybe about 23 or something. And on a Sunday morning, if we were down in Ballina on holiday, Joe used to walk up to his Aunt's place. She was the only one in the district who had a radio and he loved the Gaelic football. We'd go up with him. But to actually get up to her door, there was a set of steps, like about nine steps. So, all us kids (his kids as well, our cousins, like Mary, Madge, and me) we'd run up and down the stairs outside while they were inside listening to the football. The other kids hadn't been born at that time.

Aunt Bidney's house was nice too. They had a bed in the lounge, they had the toilet and they had the sink and

THE CONVENT AND SCHOOL

Convent of Mercy: Town School, the large building on the left

everything, a great big sink outside you know to do washing etc, a lovely garden. Just like Nan's house.

The second time I visited Nan, I was on my own. Mammy and the other kids remained in Westport. I was six years old. Nan took me to the school and I was put into third class. Sister Lourde was my teacher but I didn't like her. I was only in her class about one week when we were having a tables class. Sister Lourde asked me what three times seven was. I didn't know, so she told me to put my hand out and she came down on my poor hand with a stick. It stung, but the stinging was nothing to the embarrassment of all the other children looking at me and I didn't know any of them. I have never forgotten that 3 x 7 = 21. If I didn't have to go to school, life would have been great.

Nan's brother, Billy, had been injured in the War and had an ulcerated leg. I didn't know how Uncle Billy came to live there. All I knew was that he had a crook leg and he walked with a limp, and while Nan was dressing his leg every day, I went outside and picked dock leaves for Nan's pipe. She would put them on top of the coal range, let them get brown and then she would crush them and smoke them. When I was allowed back in, there was always a smell of Jeyes Fluid and Uncle Billy would be putting his boot back on and I could see his leg was bandaged. Uncle Billy couldn't work because of his leg and he got a pension.

James McDermott very seldom spoke to me. I knew he was Nan's husband, so I assumed that Mammy's father had died, but I was to learn later on in life that Mammy didn't have a father. James McDermott was an odd job man. He left early in the morning and didn't return until 5 o'clock or 6 o'clock at night. Sometimes he would have earned some money, but on the days he didn't earn anything, there were words between them; I mean Nan and James.

Nan would have been in her 60's. To me she looked so old. Her hair had lots of grey in it. She did her hair by gathering it together and making a bun at the top of her head. She always had black dresses and a black shawl, which she threw around her shoulders and covered some of her head as well.

Often, Nan would take me across the town. We would pass the marketplace, fruit and vegetables and fish. Nan would buy a couple of fish and if there was no one looking, she would take one and stick it in an inside pocket. I knew it was wrong but if I mentioned it, Nan would say *"These are hard times"*. Also, the same thing would happen with the gooseberries, plums or apples. One day we passed a nice house say where a doctor would live and there was a small can outside the door. The milk man would fill the can with milk early in the morning. Nan said to me *"If that milk is still there on our way back, we'll have it."* It was there and she took it. I remember her telling me that day when times are desperate you become an opportunist.

Every morning while I stayed with Nan, she would bring me a cup of tea and biscuits in bed. I was spoiled but I was getting homesick for Mammy. I also wouldn't go to school and Nan got a note from the school to say if I didn't go, they would have to let the Education Board know. I promised Nan that if she didn't show the note to Uncle Johnny, I would go to school; but going to school only lasted a few days and I stayed home again. Uncle Johnny got to know about it and

John McDermott

he used to take me. One morning, he was waiting to take me to school. I locked myself in the toilet. Eventually, after much pounding on the toilet door, I opened it. Uncle Johnny was very red in the face. I pretended to be pulling my pants up. In my ignorance, I thought Uncle Johnny would think I had just finished and not tell me off but instead, he grabbed me and made me go to school.

Shortly after that episode, I got mumps. I remember being very ill; I couldn't eat anything. James McDermott kept telling Nan to send me back to Westport. Anyway, I recovered and stayed on a while longer.

At night I wore a little vest and a little bodice with lovely little buttons down the front. When they were putting me to bed at night, they'd open the range door to let out some heat. Aunt Mamie, she'd have a big, long piece of material and it used to be up here over my head and then she'd take the hair

Bunree River, Ballina

and wind it round and I'd have ringlets the next day.

Aunt Mamie was lovely to me and to make up for me being homesick and having to go to school, she would save up some money and take me to the pictures (that's what a film was called). Mamie worked as a servant girl. She only got five shillings a week and out of that, she would give Nan some money for her board so she had very little for herself. On one occasion, Aunt Mamie collected beer bottles and got eightpence; enough to get us both in to see a film.

Sometimes at night, especially in summer, Aunt Mamie would be going out to meet her girlfriend, Mary Foy, who lived in Tyrawley Terrace, the same place as Aunt Bidney. Aunt Mamie wouldn't want to take me, but I used to perform until Nan would insist she did. I must say, Aunt Mamie never was mad at me and she coloured my lips with red paper which, when wet, would produce a nice colour and this she would use as lipstick and of course, I had to have some too.

One night, a lovely summer's evening, we went as usual to pick up Mary Foy. We walked around for a while and as it got dark, a couple of soldiers appeared. They started to chat to my aunt and Mary and it seemed as though everyone knew one another. I'm sure if I had not been there, the four of them would have gone off somewhere. Instead, they decided to go to a dance. I was all for that, except when we got to the door, everyone went in; I was last, but unfortunately I was not allowed in and so they were also asked to leave. I can imagine how they would have felt, having a spoilt child around everywhere, spoiling their fun.

Another night, Aunt Bidney gave a party. I went as usual

with Aunt Mamie. No one, by now, would say I couldn't go. Nan said for us to be home early as I had school next morning. Yuk! Anyway, we arrived at Aunt Bidney's to find the house all lit up and the music in full swing. Everyone was on the floor and a big fire burning. Someone took my hand and we went up and down the floor a few times. I got a bit bored so I asked my cousin Mary if we could boil some potatoes and have a party of our own. Mary got the pot, I peeled the potatoes and we put the pot on the hot cinders to boil. We ate them later.

The party proceeded, the poteen was going down well. "Poteen" is Irish whiskey, which is illegally distilled. It was 2.00am and we were making moves to go when Uncle Johnny arrived at the door. His face was like thunder. He ordered me and Aunt Mamie home straight away. I remember it was a moonlit night and lovely walking the two miles home, only Uncle Johnny moaned the whole way and when we got to Nan's house, there was a good argument, one thing the Irish are good at. Even though I never got to bed until around 3.00am, I was up with the lark next morning and off to school.

Uncle Johnny loved fishing in the River Moy. He caught little fish and Nan would cook them for our tea. Even though I missed Mammy a lot, I loved the life I had there with my Nan.

Behind Nan's house was a field of corn. By now I had made some friends, Tommy Ginty, Tommy Holmes, Harry Murray, Annie-Kate McLoughlin and her sister Sheila. When the corn was all cut down, we would go for a run in

Mamie McDermott

the cornfield. One day, I took off on my own. I walked quite a way; I was looking for a road that was familiar but I was going around in circles. In the end, I started to cry softly but no one was taking any notice, so I began to cry out loud. Someone came up to me and asked what was wrong. I said I was lost. Luckily, I knew the address and this kind man took me to the road I was looking for and I was on my way home. I have never forgotten what it feels like to be lost. All things come into your head like *"I'm never going to see my Nan or Mammy again"*. On other occasions, after school, we would go to the gardens and pinch apples.

Another sad thing that happened while I was in Ballina, Anthony Ginty decided to climb to the top of an old building that had been demolished, except for a brick wall quite high, and this wall had one window. Anthony climbed the wall, stood in the window and fell. He was taken to hospital and sent home apparently okay, but he began throwing up blood so all we could do was watch him die, his poor mother distraught. Anthony was buried in St Murdach's Cathedral grounds. Anthony was the brother of Tommy Ginty who I used to play with.

One day, the time came for me to go back to Westport. All in all, I had been in Ballina about one to two months. Nan put me on the bus. A chicken had come into the garden that morning and Nan decided it would be nice to send it back to Westport all plucked, of course. So, Nan grabbed the chicken, wrung its neck and when I got off the bus, I told Mammy I had a chicken in my bag. We made short work of it that night for tea.

When I got back to school in Westport, the seven year olds were preparing for First Communion. Sister Columba was the nun; she was very nice. Somehow, Mammy managed to get me a white dress and veil. I'm sure the Shanleys who had the big shop in Westport would have helped. Along came the big day. I was so excited. Mammy took me to the church; we lined up and in to Mass. Mammy had told me not to let anyone kiss me after communion because she wanted to be the first one to kiss me. I remember rushing out of the church and looking for Mammy. Out rushed Mrs Hoban from some bush, grabbed me and kissed me. Apparently it was lucky to kiss us. I suppose we were saintly or something. Anyway, Mammy was very upset. She said she would have it out with Mrs Hoban.

Decades later, my friend Briege Walsh, gave me a photo of our communion class on that day. I am the first girl in the second row.

Every three years, the Mission would come to Westport. Stalls were erected opposite the church. Different priests accompanied the Mission. Every morning and night, the Mission bells rang out. There was confession, Rosary and benediction and after three weeks, we hoped we were better people.

The O'Malleys made their money in the construction industry. They built a lot of places in Westport and were well known. In fact, the funny thing about it is that Mammy only worked for well-known people like the O'Malleys. She worked for Mr and Mrs Plunket and all of the Plunkets. They were Protestants and they lived next door to the Protestant church on the Mall. Mammy used to take me with her and that's where she plugged the vacuum cleaner in one morning into these holes and I had a hairclip in my hair and after she'd had gone into another room I poked it into the hole and it blew me across to the other side of the room. But anyway, Mammy came out screaming. I dusted myself off and I got up *"Oh my God, you could have killed yourself"* and here I am at 86.

So there was the O'Malleys, the Clancys (they had a lovely house, the Clancys), the Shanleys (they had the shop), and

Mr and Mrs Kenny. Mr Kenny was a bank manager and they had one girl called Joy. Mammy worked for all these people so when she was down and out or anything like that, they'd be the first to help her out. Joy Kenny was the same age as me so if Mrs Kenny would see Mammy in the town she'd say *"I've got something really nice belonging to Joy, Maureen can have it"* and also Mr and Mrs Regan on James Street, I used to go to school with Nuala Regan. Nuala's father was a *gardai*. Mrs Regan used to say *"Send Maureen down, I've got a lovely pinafore dress"*. I'm wearing a Regan dress in the photo I have of Mammy, and us four kids.

Danny Riley had lovely long, red hair and she was in my class at school. Sister Columba taught us and she was putting on a play, and what happened was, Sister Columba wanted a princess, so I put my hand up to be the princess, you see, and she said *"Oh yes"* (I mean, she was thinking about it) so Danny said *"But I want to be the princess with the long hair"*, so she said *"Oh Danny, you can be the princess"* and I liked the boy who was to carry the Princess on his back. His name was "Tiny Kelly" (that wasn't his real name but because he was small, his mother called him "Tiny"), and he had to carry her on his back around and we used to have to sing and it went like this:

"bi Princess breag ar capal la."

"Capal" is a horse in Gaelic. It means a lovely prince was coming along and he was going to get his princess on the horse

Nan O'Malley was one of the O'Malley children who Mammy looked after. When Nan grew up, nobody else wore trousers, but Nan did. She even went to Mass in trousers, she ignored everybody in Westport. She would do what she wanted to do. I was 7 or 8 then; that was unheard of for anyone to wear trousers. They were all in long skirts and some of the old girls wore shawls and all that.

When Dad was in the Army and I was about 7 years old, I made Mammy's life a misery for her to take her wedding ring off and give it to me. She took it off her finger and put it on mine. I was standing outside our front door. The ring fell off and went tumbling down High Street. Mammy was in a terrible state because Dad would have noticed the ring gone when he came home. Kathy Hastings found it a few days later. If Dad had found out about it, there would have been trouble.

Kathy Hastings used to bring Mammy eggs and then when Mammy peeled the potatoes (in Ireland, you never peeled potatoes until they were boiled), they were all lovely and floury and she took the skins off with a knife. Then as you peeled them, you put them back in the pot and then you got a pounder (you know, like a masher) and you'd pound them all up. So, Mammy used to peel all the potatoes and keep the peelings for Kathy's hens. She'd bring up a couple of eggs and say *"There you are, Mag"*. So, that was payment for the potato peelings.

Before that, Mammy would have sent me up the road to Mrs Mohans. Mrs Mohan used to make country butter and it was a different colour altogether and there'd be salt in it. I used to run up High Street, and maybe walk a mile and give Mrs Mohan the money for the butter and then I'd run back home, throw the butter in the pot of potatoes, Mammy would have some milk, and pound them and pound them until they were all lovely and fluffy and then Mammy would add some spring onions and with fried black pudding we would have a lovely tea.

We had no sink at all; nothing like that. In the cottages in Ballina where Nan lived, they had a little scullery and they had a big trough where you'd be able to wash the clothes.

Ireland was neutral during the War, so there was no risk of Dad being caught up to serve in the War, but he was part of Ireland's defence if Germany did choose to bomb us. I remember once in Ballina I saw a huge Red Cross on Ballina District Hospital. This was to let the Germans know it was a hospital so they wouldn't bomb it.

I would sleep with Kit, Larry and James but when Dad was away in the Army, Mammy said *"You can sleep with me"*. But in the middle of the night, she'd wake up, sit up in bed, crying to God *"Please, please God – send Jim home. I really, really miss him. Please send Jim home"* and then she'd get a headache and then she'd get one of Dad's ties and she'd tie it around her head to try to reduce the pain... and I'd be sitting up with her and she'd be saying *"Why don't you sleep?"* and I'd say *"I can't sleep 'cos you're crying"*. Mammy suffered a lot from headaches. I remember her walking down to the Quay one time because someone told her that someone at the Quay would be able to cure her.

She loved Dad. She wanted him home. And also, she felt alone because with him away, that lot (the Noones) didn't want her, but at least she had her friends down the street.

I mean, the Kirbys and then there were two sisters who were the McDonalds and they had this tiny little shop, and then next door to that was the Heratys (it's funny because they were Heratys and my grandmother's name was Heraty before she married my grandfather), and as you go down over there was the road where Mrs Kelly (and her husband was then in the Army too) lived and the Ryders, Mr & Mrs McGinn, Mr & Mrs Gibbons and then Gibbonses Pub and then Doherty's Chemist. It's like I'm almost there, I can see it like it was yesterday. Gibbonses Pub is now The Clock. Doherty's Chemist is still there.

You know the Heraty's shop, down the way? Mammy was friendly with them. Well Mr Heraty was a huge, huge man and when he died, they said *"Now, how are we going to get him down the stairs?"* because you couldn't get anyone who could carry him. They said *"I know"*, so they had two ladders outside and they took the window out. We were standing there (God knows how old I was, I'll have to remember how old I was) and so they had a stretcher or something on wood and the ones that were in the room had big ropes around the ladder and they roped him around the ladder and put him down onto High Street. He wasn't wrapped in anything. If he fell off, us kids would have said.... *"Oh God, he fell off the thing"* ... only he didn't get up. As far as we were concerned it was a great commotion and we didn't know Mr Heraty was dead.

It was Christmas Eve and the McGreevys and the Goldens was all lit up. All the lovely toys and everything used to be out there. But we never had any toys or anything. And when

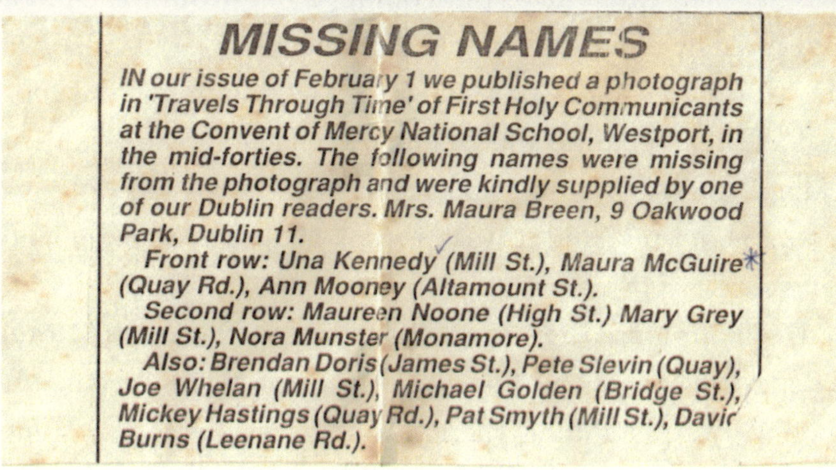

MISSING NAMES

IN our issue of February 1 we published a photograph in 'Travels Through Time' of First Holy Communicants at the Convent of Mercy National School, Westport, in the mid-forties. The following names were missing from the photograph and were kindly supplied by one of our Dublin readers. Mrs. Maura Breen, 9 Oakwood Park, Dublin 11.

Front row: Una Kennedy (Mill St.), Maura McGuire (Quay Rd.), Ann Mooney (Altamount St.).

Second row: Maureen Noone (High St.) Mary Grey (Mill St.), Nora Munster (Monamore).

Also: Brendan Doris (James St.), Pete Slevin (Quay), Joe Whelan (Mill St.), Michael Golden (Bridge St.), Mickey Hastings (Quay Rd.), Pat Smyth (Mill St.), Davic Burns (Leenane Rd.).

Communion photograph taken on steps of Convent of Mercy
Below: Names for communion photograph

Me and my granddaughter Sara in 2003, me standing in the exact same place as in the Communion photograph.

I talked to my cousin Christina (this was years later) she said *"Maureen, we didn't even know it was Christmas; Mammy couldn't buy anything. We never had anything"*, so I said *"Well, it was like that with us too"*. But coming along from the church and passing the West Hotel, McGreevys is right opposite the West Hotel and Mrs McGreevy was standing at the door and as she'd seen me and Mammy come along, she shouted *"Mag!"* and so Mammy looked over and she said *"I've got something for you"* and it was in a box about a foot and a half long.

Dad's friends were standing outside the West Hotel having a drink (as they used to). Loads of them were inside too. We were standing there, Mammy was waiting for me to go over and get the box from Mrs McGreevy and come back. I hadn't looked in the box or anything and Mammy opened the box and she saw that it was broken biscuits and she looked down at me *"Oh, what a lovely doll; oh, isn't that lovely!"* see, because my Mammy didn't want me to let on the embarrassing fact that we had been given broken biscuits on Christmas Eve. So, as we walked up Bridge Street, she said (I was as cute as) *"Oh, yeah, a beautiful doll"*. And Dad's friends would have heard and thought it was a doll.

Mammy was really onto it. Especially if she sent me off to Mrs Quinn's with the pair of shoes Mrs Mary Walsh had given to Dad, that Dad had mended. Mammy used to send me off, through the black gardens which led on to John's Row, but would be out of sight of my three Aunts' houses on John's Row. The Cusacks lived in the house between the Noones and the Blighs lived up there as well. Mammy would say *"Keep your eye out in Barrack Hill* (we used to call it Barrack Hill, not John's Row) *in case you see any of the Noones or anything like that"* and I'd go in to Mrs Quinn and she'd give me two shillings for the pair of shoes. Mammy was like selling them to Mrs Quinn. She would have met Mrs Quinn in the town and said *"I've got a pair of shoes for you"*. Now, Mrs Quinn might have somebody she could give or sell the shoes to. She used to do dressmaking and I used to play with her daughter, Kathleen Quinn. We used to have a great time around the pump just opposite our house. We used to run around the pump and be out till all hours in summer, until we were called in.

I used to love it when Mammy taught me how to tell the time. When the other kids were in bed at night, Murphys used to be open and they sold lovely jam tarts and things like that.

Mammy used to say *"Go down to Murphys and get us a jam tart"* She was teaching me the time and the clock was in the middle of the mantlepiece and we had two bulldogs either side of the mantelpiece (and I can see like yesterday that there were these two bulldogs and the clock was in the middle) and I'd come back with a jam tart. Mammy would have raked the coals and put the kettle on for a cup of tea and both of us would sit down there in front of the fire (I can see her with the clock and me beside her) and she'd say *"Before you do anything, you've got to learn 5 past, 10 past, quarter past, 20 past, 25 past, half past"* and she used to keep on until I knew that. And then she'd tell me the other side. And then she'd put the mantelpiece clock around to different times. And then the kettle would boil and then she'd make us a cup of tea and we'd sit there with our jam tart and our cup of tea. I honestly do think that I knew every single thing that ever was on her mind or happened to her or anything like that.

Mammy was either going down Bridge Street or Shop Street (I can't remember what street) but it was a street in Westport and she saw this watch on the ground so she picked it up and it was a Mickey Mouse watch and Mickey Mouse was on the front of it, but it was going. I mean today you say *"Mickey Mouse watch"* but this one was going, you know, she'd laugh (she is laughing, wherever she is, God rest her soul) but anyway. So she brought it home and she said *"Jim, I've just found a Mickey Mouse watch"* and he said *"Oh, give it here"*. Anyway she gave it to him and he said *"What are we going to do about it?"* and she said *"Well, we'll keep it because I mean how do we know who owns it"*. So, my Dad, for some reason or other, we had a little window in the kitchen, on the right-hand side of the door if you are looking at the house from High Street. He drove a nail into that side of the window frame and he hung the watch on it. It stayed there.

So one day, Philly McCarthy (she was my cousin, you know, her mother was Beazie), she came up High Street and for some reason or other, they'd bought her a watch. So, I'd go outside (because we were friends with them; we could talk to them). Mammy wouldn't worry about us going up there, it's just that they didn't like Mammy, but my Mammy never stopped us from going up and seeing Granny or anything like that. And so this day, Philly McCarthy came in and she said *"Maureen!"* and I went outside and she said *"I've got a watch"*. I said *"Oh, that's lovely"* so I went in to Mammy and I said *"Philly has got a watch"*. She said *"Oh, that's lovely. When did you get that?"* (it might be for her birthday or something – she was three years older than me, so if I was seven, she'd be 10). Mammy said *"Well, Maureen's got a watch as well"* so she climbed up on the chair and took the watch down and wound it up and Mickey Mouse goes like that, so she put it on my wrist and she said *"Now look at that. Both of you have a watch."*

I only ever wore it once, on that day. I don't know why Mammy and Dad didn't let me wear it, maybe because it was so distinctive that someone in the town might recognise it and say *"Oh, that's mine"*. On the other hand, Mammy wasn't given to jewellery. I mean, first of all, because she could never afford it. Maybe they just thought that if I wore a watch ... *"Well, if you have money to buy a watch ...You don't need any help from anyone else"*.

I'm in Sister Columba's class (I would have been seven because we have our first communion when we're seven). I used to look over the shoulder of the girl sitting next to me, maybe Nuala McGing or someone like that, for reading, until Mammy could afford to buy me a book. And if she didn't, I'd still be looking in with her. This day, Sister Columba (lovely, lovely nun), she stood up in the middle of the room and she said *"Now listen you children, I want you all to bring a penny for the black babies tomorrow. They haven't got anything to eat and they're out in Africa"*. So I went home to Mammy and I said *"Mammy, tomorrow you have to give me a penny. I've got to take it for the black babies"* and she said *"Who told you that?"* I said *"Sister Columba. I can't go to school without a penny"*. She said *"When you go to school tomorrow, you tell Sister Columba that if I had a penny, I'd buy an egg"*. God's honour, that's what she said to me. So when I went into school the next morning I told Sister Columba *"Well, my Mother would buy an egg if she had a penny but we haven't got a penny"*.

When I say the Noones wouldn't do anything for Mammy, I don't include Granny Noone in that. Granny Noone used to come down and that's when she used to throw tuppence outside the door or a penny (or whatever she had – I don't know where she got it from, because her daughters ruled the roost). There were no pensions in those days. And Granny Noone would shout *"Mag! I've just dropped a couple of pennies outside for the kids"* and then she'd walk off down the street, not come in. I don't think she ever came in because there'd be so much pressure on her from Annie and Beazie – not so much Kate.

After school, if I didn't have to pick the brambles in the back gardens for Mammy to be able to boil us the kettle in the morning before we went to school to make us a cup of tea, I'd go (as I said) to collect the meat from Mrs O'Malley or dresses from somebody or whoever was in the town that had something to give Mammy, I used to go and get it. So it was very embarrassing. But they never said anything. Even Nuala Regan whose dress I was wearing in the photo, I used to have to stand beside her. I mean, she'd maybe had it on a couple of weeks beforehand and then I've got it. But anyway, it was a dress and it was the times.

Mrs McGreal, she was on the list for me to visit and I'd have an old tin bowl and I'd hand that tin bowl to Mrs McGreal and she would give me a bowl full of dripping. So I'd take that home and that was great because we only had a quarter of butter to last us for the week on the five shillings that I had to go way out into the country to collect.

Every Wednesday I'd walk up out to Altamount Street. I'd get to this house and a woman would have a book and she would take my name and everything, then she'd give me this chit for five shillings and that had to last us until next Wednesday. And on that chit was a quarter of butter, half ounce of tea (well, maybe 8 ounces of tea or something), a loaf of bread, a pint of milk and I don't know what else. She's giving out chits (on behalf of the government) because Dad was in the Army and because the Army wages were very low. That 5 shillings was given to help Army families because if Dad wasn't in the Army he'd be lining up every Wednesday morning for the dole and it would be about 5 shillings, but because he went into the Army, they probably thought *"Well, he shouldn't lose the dole because he's doing something for the country"*. They didn't give you the dole; they made sure that these people had the *"book of chits"*, they used to call them.

I'd go into Burkes Garage after school, knock at the door of the kitchen (you'd pass all of the men as you went in and all the cars that they were mending and that) but there was a door down along the corridor and I'd knock on it and the maid would come out. I was actually in school, sitting next to these Burkes girls and I'd say *"My Mother asked me if there was anything left over after your dinner please"* and she'd say *"Hold on a minute"* and go in and she'd empty whatever was left over into a newspaper and give it to me and then I'd go home with that. Next night it would be to Mrs Charlie O'Malley on the Mall in Westport, not far from the Post Office. There, I would ask the same question and would receive nice things to eat like shepherd's pie and pieces of fresh meat which Dad would eat.

I was never free of jobs and I didn't mind it one bit. I used to really love doing it. The only thing that worried me, really, was the days that I didn't bring anything home or that I didn't bring enough kindling home for Mammy to boil the kettle for us because she used to feel very sad about that.

Bridie Swift lived across the road and she was begging after school. And I said one day to Mammy *"Mammy, would it be all right to bring Bridie Swift tomorrow?" and she said "Why? If you bring Bridie Swift, she'll be there tomorrow before you"*. I said *"Oh, I never looked at it like that"*. So there were loads of people going around begging and the people who could afford it would often give food especially to people like Mammy who knew *so* many people that I could go around and I'd never have to say anything; I'd just appear at the door and they'd give me something.

I don't know whether Dad knew I was begging. I think the begging I was doing was early on in the piece when he was working on the roads. He was definitely on the roads when I was begging. I don't think even Nan knew, only Mammy and I knew that I was begging.

When Dad went into the Army, the wages were better than working on the roads. When Dad finished in the Army it dawned on him that he could open that room at the front corner of our house and make it into a shoe-mending workshop. I think he started making a few bob because he was such a good shoemaker, I didn't have to go begging any more. It was the bottom, front left window, looking at the house from High Street.

Bridie Swift's brother was called Mattie Swift (see how it's coming back to me) and she had a little sister as well, but there was three of them there. I look back now and Mr Swift looked that old. They had an old horse and cart and he used to bring it up and down High Street (God knows what he did) but he was always out there doing whatever and she'd always be sitting at the fire and she'd have her legs like that (akimbo) and her dress sort of pulled up over her knees so that she could keep warm and we used to go over there, we'd sit down by the fire with her. Larry went over one day (he was about five so this would have been about 1940 or 1941) and he was sitting right across the way from her and all of a sudden he left and came tearing over the road and he said *"Mammy! Mrs Swift has got a big rat up her clothes"*. Mammy said *"Oh has she? Oh well, here have a cup of tea"* (or something to take his mind off the 'rat').

The Giblins lived next door to us but around the corner. There was Mr and Mrs Giblin, obviously, and they had two boys and a girl; Tommy, Petie and Mary Giblin. Tommy had the only taxi in town. We didn't call them *"taxis"*, we called them *"Hackney cars"* and he used to take people to Castlebar. Petie worked on the roads and Baby (Mary) didn't do anything; I mean I never knew about her going to school or anything like that. In the middle of the night sometimes, we used to hear dreadful, dreadful screaming. We used to wake up with this and I thought that Mrs Giblin was really beating Baby. Well, Mammy as well, she said *"I haven't got an answer to it"* but anyway we didn't find out until years later that Baby had a mental problem.

Me and Kit used to play with making mud pies and there was a big wall between their place and our place and Baby used to look over the wall and say to us *"Can I please come over and play with you?"* and about that time she would have been about 17 or something like that, and I said that she could. We would have been about seven or eight years. But there was no way of getting over – she could have gone through her front door and come along and gone in and down our garden, but we never, ever saw her playing with us. But that's the sort of mentality that the poor girl had.

Mr and Mrs Fannon just lived up near the railway station on High Street. In Ireland at that time, the men were known to have a few drinks (in fact, more than they should) and when they'd come home and maybe their tea wasn't ready or whatever, they used to get into a real argument with their wives and the next thing we knew, they were fighting and arguing and then out onto the street.

One night, Mr and Mrs Fannon ended up outside our place, fighting and arguing and she was trying to keep her shawl on and he was pulling it off her. So Mammy bolted the door and took us all upstairs and we were just looking out the bedroom window that looked out onto the street and she was getting a good belting. Mr and Mrs Fannon lived beside Mr and Mrs O'Reilly and they were another couple that were always arguing and fighting. It was Mrs O'Reilly who hid my cousin Lil when the authorities came to find out where she was and why she wasn't at school. She hid in a window seat and the top lifted up.

The Ryders lived on the other side of the road and they had dolls because their mother and father had a shop. They brought the dolls over to our side of the street and we were sitting on the steps (you know, there were steps as you walked down High Street) and we were looking at the dolls (me and Kit) but we couldn't play with them; they were playing with them and we were looking at them.

Just across the road were the McGings, they were quite well-off and Mrs McGing sent her daughter over to collect me and Kit and we were taken up into this room and she said to me *"My children have grown up and I haven't got any dolls but I have got something that I think that you and your sister can play with"* so we were very excited, we thought *"What is it?"* so she comes in with a round thing (it wasn't marble but it was like that; it was black and shiny, heavy) and there were holes all around it and we looked at it. It was like a plate but about two inches thick.

And then she went off and Kit and I were looking at each other 'cos we couldn't see what this was that we were going to get. She came back with about six or seven little candles and she put the candles into the holes and then she got a box of matches and she lit the candles (and we were still looking there) and she said *"Now this is lovely because you can sit down and you can take it home with you and you can play with it"* (we were about six and seven then) and we said *"Thank you very much"* and we walked out.

We ran up High Street and into Mammy's. She said *"What have you got there?"* and we said *"Well, Mrs McGing invited us into her house. She has a lovely house on the inside and she's got a daughter and she sent her over because the Ryders were playing with the dolls and we weren't allowed to touch them so she said that we could do this instead of having dolls"*. So Mammy said *"So what is it?"* I said *"What you do is, you get all these candles out and you put them in them little holes"*. Then I took the box of matches out of my pocket and she said *"What are you doing?"* I said *"I've got to light the whole load of candles and then we can sit down and we can have a good look at them"* ... she said *"No. If I'm here, you can play with them all the time but if I'm not here, I'd have to hide the matches because it's very dangerous. God Almighty, what was she thinking of?"* and I said *"Well, I think she felt sorry for us because we didn't have a doll"*. Anyway, I don't think we ever saw it again or if it was ever lit up again. Mammy might have taken our minds off it by buying us a little book or telling us a story or whatever. So that was that.

The Kitricks (good friends of Mammy's) had an old guy there called Piety Gibbons and one day I stopped there and Mrs Kitrick gave me a bit of bread and jam, or a bit of bread and butter and sprinkling of sugar or something like that. I'd sit outside on a cushion (I remember that so well) and eat the bread and jam and then come down home. One day I went up there (I must have been about eight at the time, so 1941 or 1942) and old Piety Gibbons was always sitting just across the way and so I went in and I couldn't see anyone around. And so he says *"Come over here"* so I went over to him and he was looking at me and said *"Here, sit up here on my lap"*, so I sat up on his lap and he said *"Show me your knickers"* and the minute he said *"Show me your knickers"* I jumped off his lap and ran down the road and I told Mammy *"Piety asked me ..."*. Right, she said! So I never went up there again; she wouldn't let me. She said *"If there's nobody around there, don't go in"*, but you know they never say why or what would happen.

You walked everywhere in them days. You never thought anything of it. There were no buses. I've told you about the one car in Westport, the *"Hackney Car"* owned by Tommy Giblin. He used to bring people the ten miles to Castlebar, for the boxing, going back and forward until he'd taken them all. If anyone wanted to go to the hospital to see anyone, it was his cab that you got. He wouldn't have made much money out of it but that was his living.

When Nan came to Westport, she caught the bus and I used

to go and get her from the bus stop outside the Railway Hotel. We would stop at Gibbonses pub at the bottom of High Street, by the clock. She wouldn't drink anywhere else. She'd leave me outside and say *"Stand there, amock."* – It was another way of saying "darling" or something like that, or *"asthore"* she might say. She'd go in on her own and get a pint of Guinness and she'd sit in there and she wouldn't care who's there, you know; she'd just sit there. And then she'd remember that I was outside and she'd come out and she'd say *"Here you are"* and I'd say *"I don't want any Nan". "Have a drink. It's good for you!"* So, she'd put it up to my mouth and I'd end up with a great froth and I never knew that I ended up with a froth. And we walked indoors and Mammy said *"Mother! You've tried to give Maureen Guinness again!"* and she'd say *"Oh, it's good for her"*. Mammy said *"So, you stopped on the way?" "Oh, yes, always have my pint of Guinness"*.

Nan didn't give a toss about anybody. I mean, the Noones might not even exist; she never worried when she crossed the road to the pump to get the water, went down the town, the road, with her shawl wrapped round her. That probably used to brass them off because Granny Noone never wore a shawl. Granny Noone was always dressed in beautiful clothes you know, lace and things like that. But Nan, she wore the same old clothes all the time. She wore old shoes with black stockings and she doubled up the stockings in the garter. Nan's hair was a dark brownish colour with some grey hairs. She had long hair that she always wore in a bun at the top of her head. She rolled it round and round and then stuck a hairpin in it. She looked poor and she was poor.

Nan smoked dock leaves in a pipe. The minute that she sat down and she was happy with herself, she'd take her old pipe out and bang it down against something to get any stuff out of it and then she'd fill it up. And I always remember her pressing the roasted dock leaves down into her pipe, pressing it down again and then she'd light it and sit there and smoke all these dock leaves.

Nan was pretty lucky because she had a big coal range. They'd boil the kettle on it. But when she came up to our place, all we had was an open fire with a long piece of iron rod and then you'd hang the iron pot on it. I used to collect the dock leaves but for her to do those dock leaves at our place, it would have been a big job because we'd put them all into the oven and she'd have to keep a good eye on them, you know, because they'd burn on the bottom. Whereas, in her house, she could dry them by spreading them out on the top of the range. When I was in Nan's house in Ballina, I'd come in with the bundle of dock leaves and she'd cut the stalks off them, and then she'd cut them up and put them all around the top of the range and turn them over every now and then to see that they were all getting lovely and crispy and then when that was done, she'd take them all out, put something on the table, like a newspaper, and chop them all up fine. And it looked like tobacco. That's what she did and then she'd press them down into her pipe.

There were three schools in Westport. The National School was a primary school that you would attend if you were just an ordinary kid growing up in Westport. The Industrial School was a primary school that you would attend if you were in the orphanage. The Sacred Heart School was a secondary school. Kit and I went to the National school, also known as the Town school. It was in the grounds of the Mercy Convent on Altamount Street, about two miles from High Street, and we walked there and back in hail, rain or snow, often arriving wet and cold. Sometimes, our outer garments were taken off us and dried, but our shoes and socks were soaked and we stood in these all day.

I was seven years old and in Sister Columba's class. We often used to go to school, as I said, without anything inside us because Mammy couldn't make the fire up. Mammy always tried to give us something to eat before we went to school but sometimes there wouldn't be enough kindling wood to boil a kettle and she would be sad watching us go off hungry. My job was, after school each day, to gather kindling wood. Sometimes I got a bagful but other times, I didn't do so well. Consequently, the fire would go out.

And we'd be coming out (because there was a break at about 10 o'clock) for a play in the yard and go to the toilet and Big Sister Dominic (who was a great nun) – she was in charge of the Infants. All I remember about her is that she had all the dolls on the top shelf and there's a sandpit, so you had a lovely time when you went to school at three years of age in Ireland, just to play in the sandpit and then you'd go into Sister Mary Mercy's and she'd read you a book. Each year you'd go into a new class. And soon you'd go to Sister Bernadette's where she decided that she was going to pin my lips together with the safety pin one day if I didn't be quiet, and I was absolutely beside myself, but it never happened.

When we got our break at 10 o'clock, the doctor's and policeman's children, they'd come down the stairs and Sister Dominic would come out and she'd call all these children by their names and they'd all go into that classroom and they'd all have a lovely cup of hot chocolate because their parents brought the chocolate to Sister Dominic and all she had to do was put the hot water and the milk in. And all us children we'd all be ushered down these steps and out into the freezing cold. I often used to think about that when you'd see it but it's nobody's fault, it's just how things are. We'd come out of there and we'd see the "orphans" (as we used to call them) up the other end. There was no partition fence. The kids just knew what end they should play in.

The country children had to come to school from five to six miles away, some from Caillte Mách and they were really wet. If it was Lent and we arrived at school without going to Mass, we got the strap unless we had a good reason.

The Sisters of Mercy Convent had a House of Mercy on the convent grounds where families that didn't have a lot of food could go every evening at about four o'clock, after the cows were milked. These families could come to the House of Mercy and collect skim milk, that's milk with the cream taken off. I was in the queue most nights with my can and walked carefully all the way home so we could all have a drink of milk with our mashed potatoes and onions. Mrs McGreal lived on the Newport Road. She used to collect the dripping from her roasts for us and that was another of my jobs, to call in with an empty bowl and receive a full one.

I have already said that Kit, Larry, James and I used to

sleep in the same bed, a four-poster with a straw mattress. Mammy and Dad slept in another bed opposite us. Margo slept in the cot as she was only two years old and later, after Tom was born, he slept with Mammy and Dad. One night *"The Children of Mary"* called at our house. They were in charge of distributing charitable funds. Mammy took them upstairs and showed them where we slept. Mrs Mulligan was one of them. Mammy tried to draw attention to the fact that four of us were sleeping in the one bed, not enough blankets and no sheets, but the Children of Mary were not a charitable organisation and nothing much came of that.

CHAPTER THREE

1940 - 1942 My Mother Contracted TB

In about 1940, when I was about seven years old, I remember Dad coming home from the Army on compassionate leave. Mammy probably wasn't feeling good in herself and she knew there was something wrong with her because she wasn't as mobile or didn't have the energy she used to have.

I remember one day Mammy saying *"Jim"* and I didn't hear any more of what she said but they opened the door leading onto that room by where my Dad used to mend the shoes. This is the room Mary Salmon used to rent. She told Dad what to do and he reached up to a tall shelf and he took down a salt shaker, a little round glass container. In Ireland, we didn't have salt and pepper shakers. We got salt in bulk and then you put them into little cellars. You got the salt out with a spoon or your fingers. So, when Dad took the salt cellar down off the shelf, I had a look at it but all I could see was like if someone had spat in the salt cellar, but Mum said *"There's blood in it, there's blood in it"*. I didn't know what TB was. I just thought *"Might she have a cold?*" or *"Why is that happening?*" So, I reckon it was from then that Mammy knew she had TB.

Mammy never smoked. Mammy looked after a household where one of the men had TB. It was Mammy's job to change his bed and wash his clothes and that's how she caught the disease, or so I was told.

In autumn 1941 (about September) Mammy took us kids to Ballina. This was my third visit to see my Nan. The corn was high in the field across the road and along from there was a paddock with two white horses in it. Nan came in very excited and said *"Mag come out there's two white horses in the field."* We all went outside. To us it was just two white horses but Nan and Mammy both thought it was lucky to see a white horse and no doubt they were hoping it might cure Mammy of TB. Later that month we returned to Westport.

In February 1942, Mammy was about to give birth and I was sent to get the midwife. I ran down High Street and the back shops and knocked at Mrs O'Malley's door. Mrs O'Malley had a raised mole on her face. I'll always remember. I can see her. I wish I could see Mammy's face as clearly as I can see this woman's face. I told her Mammy was going to have her baby and then we both came back to the house. Dad must have been on compassionate leave. He put a *put-you-up* downstairs and him and I slept there. Mammy gave birth to a boy on 14th February 1942 and she named him Thomas Joseph Mary. I think Mammy added 'Joseph' and 'Mary' becuase she knew she was going to die and she was asking Joseph and Mary to look after Tom. Tom was born with TB.

Mrs O'Malley stayed all night with Mammy, and Tom

was born probably about two or three in the morning. I heard his first cry the day he was born and I was with him, 64 years later, the night he died, in Boyup Brook, near Perth in Western Australia.

The War was still on. The Army pay wasn't a lot and with six children by now, Mammy's health was failing. I was nine years old and did my best to help with minding my brothers and sisters while Mammy scrubbed floors and did housework around the town. I don't know how long I was away from school (quite a while because I remember doing odd jobs, looking after James and Larry and Margo) and the next thing was that Guard Kearns arrived at the door. He knew me and he says *"Oh Maureen, is your Mammy in?"* and I said *"She is but she's very ill in bed"* so he went up with me and he said *"Mrs Noone, I'm really sorry to see you in the state that you're in but I'm sent on a job and it's that you're keeping Maureen away from school and I'm sorry but she'll just have to go back to school"*. And she said *"All right, that will be okay"*.

I used to go a lot to the Doctors Clinic. Dr Walsh was there. I'd be sitting on the seat in the clinic and then I'd see all the bottles up on the top shelf and they were all clean. When I went in there, he made a mixture up for me and I used to take it back up to Mammy. Now, that could be for her chesty cough (I don't know) but that's what I used to do.

I also remember one night Mammy wasn't well and she said to me *"Can you go and get Dr Walsh?"* and I said *"Yes"*. I knew where he was; he lived up in Altamount Street. And I ran down High Street and up Altamount Street. So, I knocked on the door and he came to the door and I said *"My Mother's not well and she wants to see you"* and then he said *"Hold on a minute, I'll get my bag"* and him and I walked all the way back. When he came in, he examined her but whether he told her or whether she knew that there was nothing they could do with her, her lungs were kaput.

Sometimes, in the middle of the night when Mammy was really ill, I used to have to get up and if the fire had gone out in the room upstairs, I used to have to get it sorted, so I could boil the kettle and make her a cup of tea.

Dad took leave from the Army, without permission. He told Mammy *"They'll be coming for me. So we have to be on the lookout"*. Dad told me *"If ever you see a green van* (not a car, a green van) *coming up High Street, tell me because I'll have to make a quick getaway up to bed"*. As luck would have it, I was standing at the door one day or out in the street playing and I saw this green van coming up. I roared in the door and I said *"Dad, there's a green van coming up High Street"*. I've never seen anyone jump over the counter so fast. He could have left his worktable through the door. He was there, he was mending shoes and he just jumped over the counter, into the kitchen, up the stairs and then we pretended we didn't know the Army was there.

So, there was a knock at the door and Mammy went to the door and *"Is James Noone here?"* and she said *"Yes, he is". "Can we see him?" "Yes you can, but he's in bed, he's not very well"*. They said *"It's all right, we've brought a doctor with us"*. As Mammy was walking up the stairs, every two steps she'd take, she'd turn around and say something, so as to give Dad a bit more time to get into bed. And I was after her, I was right behind her looking at them so they had me to contend with as well. So we got up and Dad was in bed and we stood at the end of the bed and the doctor went up and said to him *"I'll just examine you"* and he said *"Oh yeah, you're poorly all right. You've got a fast heart rate and you don't look well and all that but we're taking you back. We've got to take you back because you're absent without leave"*. He said *"Well, I'm sick and Maggie's not well"* ["Maggie", that rings a bell, that's what he called Mammy] *"So, yeah, I'll come"*. He got dressed and they put him into the green van and off they went. And that's when Mammy really got herself down and every night she just sat up in the bed. I went into her bed with her while Dad was away. She cried her eyes out and prayed to God to send Dad home.

Mammy would go to Mass different times during the week. She would pray at the statue of the Virgin Mary at the back, left of St Mary's on the Mall. She couldn't always get to Mass on a Sunday when us kids were little but I do remember one Sunday she took me. And about this time she mustn't have been feeling very well because she said to me *"I'm going to go into the sacristy and I'm going to open the door there* [like into the church] *and I'm going to hear Mass from there"* and I was with her and I think it was because she thought that if she wasn't well or anything, she could just walk down the corridor and go out of the church without anybody seeing her. I don't remember Mammy coughing in fact I didn't know she had TB. When she used to be lying in bed, I'd often say to her when she would tell me to rake the coals and make her a cup of tea, I often used to say *"Mammy, can you just come down; can you just come downstairs?"* and she'd say *"I can't"*. She had a big stick by her bed and she used to bang it when she needed me to go up and help her but there were days when Mammy would come down and get dinner ready for us. They were great days.

There were no cinders but as the turf burnt down, if you raked the coals it used to come all red hot again. And then you'd put another few little bits of turf on it and then later on you'd scoop a few bits of coal. The coal man used to come and under the stairs was all the coal so I knew where to get that. The turf would be all dry, you know, because the guy would bring a bag of turf and that would be under the stairs as well. And we used to love the bits where you could break it off; there was some turf that was really hard, like coal, it used to get that hard but the bits that you could break off, that's what we used to use to make the embers come alive and then throw a little bit of coal on that; in no time at all, you'd have a lovely big fire in the room. In fact, I think the fire was on all the time when Mammy was lying in bed, from what I can gather, because it was very easy for me to put the kettle on the hot cinders and make her a cup of tea on the fire in her bedroom.

One day Mammy was so ill in bed. She said to me *"Go down*

to Mrs McNamees and ask them for a penny halfpenny and then go on to the West Hotel and buy me a shortbread biscuit" and I thought that was great because she's going to eat something because she was just lying there, fading away. So I went down to Mrs McNamee, she gave me the penny halfpenny, I went to the West Hotel, I got Mammy the biscuit, I went back, raked the coals, made her a cup of tea, gave her the biscuit and then a few days after that, I don't know what got into me but I thought to myself *"I would like a biscuit"* so I did the same thing, went down to Mrs McNamees, said *"Oh Mrs McNamee, my Mammy said could you give her another penny halfpenny"* and she said *"Sure I'll give Mag a penny halfpenny".* I said *"I'm going to get her another shortbread biscuit"* and she said *"Yeah, yeah, that's fine"* so I went into the West Hotel and I bought the shortbread biscuit and I ate it.

When Mammy made an effort to come downstairs, she was worried that the four of us who were going to school were going with no breakfast. She went to the convent and saw the Nun in charge of the Alms. Mother Aidan assured Mammy we would get a breakfast if we came to the House of Mercy kitchen early in the morning. Kit and I did go about twice or three times. We received two slices of bread with rhubarb jam and two mugs of tea. We sat in a room with nuns coming in and out. One in particular, Sister Juliana (God rest her soul) she pulled the bell for 9.00am school. So, if we were still there, Sister Juliana came to ring the bell, and we left hurriedly for our classroom. We didn't want our friends to see us coming from the orphanage side. We hated the smell of the food, not homely, we hated everything about it.

I'd be getting on towards nine now and I'd be upstairs in Sister Lewis' class. Everyone couldn't stand Sister Lewis because you didn't have to do much and you put your hands out and she had a stick that was about a foot long but round at the top and then it petered off at the end. And when she whacked you (especially on a cold morning) I mean your poor old hands. But anyway, she was my teacher then.

By this time, Mammy was really getting very ill and could hardly come downstairs. I used to say to Mammy *"Why don't you come down?"* and she'd say *"Make me a cup of tea"* and I'd make her a cup of tea. I'd say *"Why can't you just come down? It would be lovely if you came down"*, and she'd say *"I can't come down"* and I'd say *"Okay, then"*. She said to me *"You have to stay away from school because I haven't got anyone to look after the kids or anything like that"* and I said *"Yes, I'll stay away from school; I don't mind"*. I probably didn't have a school book to read anyway, so that was good.

Nan come up again from Ballina to help Mammy. Mrs Kelly from the Cottages came down (because she used to wash our clothes and see us off to school, so it might be her that would be making Mammy a cup of tea) but when I was home I was with Mammy all the time; I never left her at all. I wouldn't leave her for any reason.

In June 1942, Mammy went into the Creagh Sanatorium in Ballinrobe for the first time, with Tom. I think it was around this time when Dad (God rest his soul) was in the kitchen mending shoes and he had that big lamp on the wall and we were going to bed and he said *"Oh, better take the little lamp up with you"* so he lit it for us and brought it up to the bedroom (I can see him putting it on the mantelpiece) and we went into bed but Kit and I wouldn't stop laughing. Larry, James and Margo were asleep. I can remember Dad coming up because we were laughing and giggling, and he took the lamp away and we were in the bloody dark! So that shut us up.

Dad put us three girls in the Orphanage, just temporarily while Mammy was away. The Orphanage was in the grounds of Mount Saint Mary's Convent of Mercy, in Altamount Street. I remember actually going in and we were allowed to wear our own clothes; we weren't given orphanage clothes or anything like that. So we got in there and the first thing I knew was that this tall girl came along. Her name was Rita Reddington; there were four Reddington sisters and Rita Reddington was about 14 (as you know, I was nine and Kit was seven and Margo was nearly three). So, Rita took us aside and she said that she was going to look after us and that we would be in the last four. I didn't know what *"the last four"* was, but I just went *"Yeah, okay"*. So, what *"the last four"* was, the dressing room was halved and there was four classes of, say, eight or nine children on one side of the dressing room, and there were four classes of nine children (or whatever) on the other side of the room. What that meant is that on a Wednesday, say, the first four classes, they had a bath and the last four classes didn't. So, then on the next Wednesday, the last four classes had a bath and you didn't. So, we had a bath once a fortnight.

The thing was that, when I looked around and I could see them all with grey flannel dresses and petticoats on, and we were allowed to keep ours, I thought to myself *"Well, my Mother is in hospital and I know that we're going to go home because Dad said 'The Nuns are going to look after you and when your Mother comes home, I'm going to come and pick you up'"*, so, we were quite happy about that. Me and Kit were in Rita Reddington's class and we were in the last four. Margo was three years old and was looked after by an older girl.

All I know is that I hated it; I didn't like it at all because I was nine years of age and I couldn't go and see my friends down in the Town school or anything like that. I was up in the Industrial School which was adjacent to the National School, both in the Convent grounds, but there was different nuns. We weren't in there long; I would say two weeks to three weeks we were in there and one day Dad came up and the nuns took us out and we were all washed and we had our clothes on and we went home and we were that happy that Mammy was home from the hospital.

She was walking around and doing bits and pieces. She hadn't actually gone to bed and stayed in bed at that time. Just after she got out of the hospital, she must've gone down to the O'Malleys. I know this because in 1974 when Don and I went to Westport we went to see Nan O'Malley. Nan said *"Well, I'm going to tell you something. The first time your mother went into the hospital and you went into the orphanage, she saw me and she said 'I know what's going to happen; they'll be put into the orphanage. Now I'm home, they're out of the orphanage. I know I'm dying and what I want to ask you is could you please, when Maureen is 16, because they'll never be able to come out until Maureen is 16, could you go to the orphanage and tell Mother Evangelist (or whoever is there at the time) that I have said to you that I want Maureen to learn hairdressing so she can look after the others'"*.

I don't clearly remember Mammy leaving the house to go to Ballinrobe for the second and last time. This was in August 1942. It was early in the morning (because we were all there). I mean, Dad never said she was going to not come back or anything, he just said that *"Your Mother had to go to the hospital again"* and he never said anybody was going into the orphanage.

I know that she walked down High Street and Bridge Street and that she stood at that bus stop outside the Railway Hotel on the Mall and I do know the last person that saw her. In 1974, my husband Don and I were in Westport. I said to Don *"I have to see Delia Ford"* and he said *"Well, where is she?"* I said *"I know where she is"*. And would you believe it, all them years gone by, she had a little pub (you wouldn't call it a *"pub"*, you know .. when you walked in, it was probably as big as that kitchen) and she lived upstairs and there was one person sitting at the counter, having a drink and Delia Ford was behind the bar, sitting down and talking to this guy.

Don and I walked in. I said *"Hello, I know you"* and she says *"Oh"* and I said *"Your name is Delia Ford, isn't it?"* and she said *"Well, you do know something"* – the exact words that she said to me *"You do know something"* and I said *"Do you remember my Mother, Margaret Noone?"* and she said *"Oh Maggie! Oh, you're not Maureen are you?"* and I said *"Yes, I am. I've just come to ask you if you can tell me a bit about my Mother"* and she said *"Oh, one of the best people that I've ever known. We were really good friends. You know, things were hard. The awful thing about it was, as you know, the Noones didn't want you so you ended up in the orphanage and everybody was sad about that at the time"* and she said *"Do you know something? I was the last person to see your Mother. She was standing by the bus stop with the baby and she was on her way to Ballinrobe Sanitorium."*

Being as Tom was only seven months old and he had TB as well, he went with her to Ballinrobe. Dad got out of the Army on compassionate grounds to look after us.

One morning I was in Sister Lewis' class and Sister Lewis stood up and said *"We've just heard the sad news that Maureen Noone's mother has died and we'll say a prayer for her"*. I found out at the same time as all my classmates. It came as a terrible shock. I didn't believe it. I didn't realise what happened after that. I was just so in shock but Kit tells me that Mary Noone (our cousin, who was nine years older than me – she was 18 then and worked as a servant girl for the Smiths on Mill Street), she was sent up to the convent to get us. Kit tells me that Mary Noone said *"I don't know what's going to happen to you children now"* or *"you two now because your Mother is not here anymore and it's not going to be the same"* and Kit said *"When I look back on it, I thought 'She could have been a bit more kind to us'"* but that's what Kit told me when I went to London. She said *"Mary Noone wasn't very nice; she came and got us and told us all the way home what we had to do"*. Mammy died on 26th September 1942.

In 2003, I went to Westport with my daughter Margaret, my grand-daughter Sara, and my niece Marina (Kit's daughter). There were a few nuns still living in the convent and after a search they found the key to the school building. We went up the stairs and into the classroom where Sister Lewis announced that my Mammy had died.

The only time I remember Granny Noone being in our

house was on the day my mother died. I remember my father standing, leaning on the mantelpiece with his head bowed and Granny was comforting him. I never saw her at any time in our house before or after that day. I believe she was too scared of her daughters to come down.

It was around this time that Annie, Katie and Beazie came into our house for the first time. There wasn't going to be a wake *"because she died in Ballinrobe."* I don't know why Mammy dying in Ballinrobe meant there wouldn't be a wake. Annie told me to go up to the Convent and ask Sister Aidan for a 'habit' to lay my mother out in. So far as I was aware, a habit was what nuns wore but I went up to the convent and asked Sister Aidan. She said she didn't have any habits but she gave me a nightdress. Nan came up from Ballina and she was looking after us. When she saw the nightdress she said *"Leave it, your Mammy can be buried in whatever she's wearing."*

To me, there was no way that we were going to go in the orphanage 'cos now Nan was going to look after us, and that was it. Tom was sent from Ballinrobe to a hospital or a sanatorium in Tuam. He never came home.

The Navins made the coffin and Mammy's body was brought from Ballinrobe and put into the coffin. The coffin was in Navin's hearse. We all went to St Mary's Church and the funeral service was there.

We got Tommy Giblin from next door to come round in his Hackney cab. I got into the car with Nan, Aunt Bidney, and Aunt Bidney's daughter (my cousin) Christina, who was only about two years old. Aunt Bidney left her other children in Ballina. Joe Moyles, their father, must have been looking after them. There was also Mrs Kitrick (who was a good friend of Mammy's) in the car.

Someone asked my Dad *"What's going to happen to you?"* and he said *"I'm going to walk behind the car"*. So, there was a lot of people walking in the funeral procession (because that's what they did at the time). They couldn't afford cars. There was only, like I said, one car in the town. So, there were all these people with us in the car, following the hearse and Dad. I don't know about Kit, Larry and James, I can't remember where they were that day. Mrs Kirby lived down the road, Mum was really very friendly with her. I think Mrs Kirby would have taken Margo because she wasn't three years old at that time. So, the kids must have gone somewhere. We followed the hearse and everyone walked behind the hackney cab to Aughaval Cemetery. It's a good few kilometres. To the best of my recollection, Annie, Katie and Beazie did not come to Mammy's funeral or burial.

The drive was slow and when we got there, the hearse went into the cemetery and they took Mammy's coffin out of the back. They told me to sit in the car, so I never got out of the car but I remember seeing Mammy's coffin being lowered down into the grave and I had Christina on my lap and that was it. A lot of people went on, obviously, and they were around the grave and they said all the prayers and what have you. I was sitting in the back seat, I think, on that side looking into the cemetery. It was quite close to the gate.

I should say here that I spent many years trying to locate Mammy's grave. When I did locate it, in 2003, it was nowhere near the gate. It turns out that the gate was in a different position in 1942 when Mammy died.

I can't remember much about it afterwards. I think Nan and me and all of us kids were together in our house with Dad and Nan just looked after us, gave us our tea and we were all happy (as happy as you could be) but because Nan was there it made a real difference, someone that loved us, you know.

By the time Mammy died when she was 32 and I was nine, I could do most things. But the thing is this, that I always thought if I was 15 and Mammy had died, I'd have kept everyone together. But at nine, it was out of my hands because Aunt Anne on the hill came down and said *"All you children have to go into an orphanage because there's nobody to look after you"*.

A few days after Mammy died, Nan and Aunt Bidney took me back to Ballina with them. I don't know why they only took me. Maybe because they thought I was most affected because I was the oldest. Maybe because taking one of us took some load off Dad. Lil Noone my cousin who was 15 moved in to look after the rest of the family in High Street. I didn't have a coat. Aunt Mamie had an oatmeal coat. There was a dressmaker and they got her to make a coat out of it for me. I loved it.

When I came back to Westport after being in Ballina for two months I felt a bit left out. There was Lil, Kit, Larry, James and Margo and they were all playing games and singing songs. One song was about Sierra Sue *"I'm sad and lonely the rocks and hills are longing to sierra sue for you I'm lonely"*. I didn't know the song. They were playing a game with their hands and I didn't know it. I arrived with my suitcase and my bags with the chicken and other little things that Nan had put together and I think they were a bit jealous of me. It took me a little while to fit back in.

But in the meantime, Dad was paying Mrs Kelly from the Cottages in the Quay five shillings a week to do our washing. She never combed our hair or seen that we were okay that way, she just did the washing and maybe cooked a meal for us. And five shillings at that time was a lot of money.

CHAPTER FOUR

1942 - 1946
Into The Orphanage

To be left with six children, the oldest nine years of age, must have been terrible. It's only now when I look back that I can see my Dad had to put us in the orphanage.

So in November 1942, Dad decided he could look after Larry and James but us three girls, he couldn't manage. I remember Aunt Annie Noone coming to our house to get us ready. All our clothes had to be washed and we got new vests. Aunt Annie put a sheet of newspaper on the floor and I was first to have my hair combed for lice, then Kitty and Margo. Margo was only three years old. We got dressed and Dad walked us to the orphanage. As we walked up the path, I remember feeling sad. Mammy would never have wanted this. We were met by a nun and ushered into a big room. We said goodbye to Dad; he promised to come and see us. We were lucky that the orphanage was in Westport.

The orphanage was in the grounds of the Convent of Mercy, the only convent in Westport. The Convent was where the nuns lived. That's the main building. It faces Altamount Street and is the first building you notice when you look up, through the front gates, from the street. It was

on the steps of this building where I had had my photograph taken on the day of my First Holy Communion. There is a convent kitchen where orphans, if they reach sixteen and no one comes for them or they don't know what to do with them, they'd be sent up to the nuns' kitchen and then they're washing pans etc. In the same grounds is the orphanage and the orphanage school (the Industrial School).
A nun by the name of Sister Elizabeth was in charge of the children. We were taken to the bathroom and told to strip. Our hair was examined. They found nits. We had our bath, then Sister Elizabeth rubbed paraffin oil into our hair. The smell was terrible. Once dressed, we were taken to Sister Columbus' room, sat by the fire. John Malone, who was a handyman around the Convent, came into the room and seeing us with our hair drenched in paraffin oil, said *"Don't sit too near that fire; you might catch alight"*.

In the days that followed, we were measured for the uniform that we would wear until one day we would be free to leave - whenever that would be. The material was grey flannel. Kitty and I got a grey flannel dress each and a grey flannel petticoat. It was winter, so I'm sure looking back, we would have been warm. Margo, only being three years, got clothes more suitable for a baby.

There were about 80 children in the orphanage, all there for different reasons. Mostly, their parents were dead or, like us, one parent was alive but didn't wish to look after the children. There were the older girls, say about 14 years old. They would be responsible for seven children, seeing the children were dressed properly, also making sure we were

School house
(The classroom window is the nearest, on the top floor. This is all that remains of the large town school building)

clean. Kitty and I were put into Nora O'Connor's class. She was a nice girl and she was nice to Kit and me.

There were 76 beds in St Joseph's dormitory, seven rows with ten beds and the odd bed here and there. The door on the right hand side was the fire escape. In my time, the beds were not so bunched up but I think when the photo was taken, nearly all the orphans had left. We used to polish the floor until we could see our faces in it.

Our day started with the bell ringing at 6.00am; everyone out of bed and prayers, then out to the bathroom. Wooden floors and cold water. After washing our hands and faces and

Me in the classroom in 2003

cleaning our teeth with salt, we made our beds. At 7.30am we lined up and went to Mass, every morning – hail or rain or snow. After Mass, breakfast; a bowl of porridge and cup of tea, then off to school. At 12 noon we had lunch, half hour play time, then school until 3.00pm, a snack of two pieces of bread and dripping and one cup of cocoa.

At 3.30pm everyone had to assemble in the dressing room. The girl in charge of us would fine-comb our hair and if we had nits, she would get rid of them. Kitty would pull my nits out and I would do the same for her. On Wednesday afternoon we would change our knickers and vests. We had to wear our underclothes for one week. Our grey petticoat and grey flannel dress was worn for nine months.

The orphanage had flushing toilets. There were two cubicles in this big toilet place.

The next photograph is of Tom Navin with some of the orphans. Tom was a builder from Mill Street. Tom and his son John-Tom used to come up to the orphanage and do maintenance work. None of the kids in this photograph would know who they were or who belonged to them. They were told nothing. A lot of orphans came from Dublin and were the children of the Yanks who were stationed in Dublin at the time. I can name most of them. Mary and Annie Knight were twins. Mary Knight got the job of looking after all the babies that were sent from Dublin. My friend Josie Rogers, is standing on the right of Tom Navin and my friend Annie Maughan is marked with an "X".

It was really sad for Kit and I because we had made friends in the National School but now that we were in the orphanage, we had to go to the Industrial School. We could see our friends playing in their end of the playground but we had to keep to our end. One day I saw a girl in the Town School part of the playground wearing my oatmeal coat.

If you were in the orphanage and studying at the Industrial School and if your mother or father (if they were alive) or one of your relatives was paying five shillings a week, you would have a nice jumper and skirt and when you got your School Certificate at age 16 (in the Industrial School), you were sent from the Industrial School to the Sacred Heart School if it was thought you were brainy enough. You'd open the back gate and you'd walk out to the Sacred Heart School and there you got taught all sorts of things to go out into the world, like shorthand typing or whatever it was.

But it wasn't for most of us, it was only for the ones who had someone to pay for that. My friend Teresa, her mother paid extra for her and she could have gone to the Sacred Heart School but she didn't want to go, she wanted to be a nun. If you were in the Sacred Heart School and you were going to work in the Irish government, you had to speak Irish fluently, and you would study that.

The ordinary kids in the town (not orphans) would attend the Sacred Heart School after obtaining School Certificate at the Town School. People like Burkes Garage, the guard's daughter, Nuala O'Regan and the Kennedys, because we mixed with all them kids who had the money and they would all decide what they wanted to do with their lives and that was the next place they'd go but not all took up the opportunity.

As Christmas Day 1942 was looming, there was great activity going on, especially amongst the older girls. Their names were called out at night when we were all off to bed at 7.30pm. The older girls stayed behind; it was all very secret. The stage was erected with a lovely backdrop of a wood and lovely green trees and flowers. Then in the middle of December we were told we were going to have a concert. Nuns were invited and the older girls danced and sang and put on a play. It lasted about two hours and it was great fun.

Then Christmas Day arrived, Santa was coming. Everyone would get a doll (that's what the older girls were doing at night, making dolls) – drab body but nice faces. We would play with these dolls for hours. Storybooks were provided, Grimm's Tales and we would sit and read over the Christmas period. Christmas Day was lovely. We got a nice dinner and custard and jelly and an apple.

Kitty, Margo and I were called for, told we got a parcel from a Mrs Kenny, and that we could choose something so we chose a bar of chocolate and were told we could get the rest later. It's a pity Christmas wasn't every day.

On 26th December, men got dressed up. We used to call them "Mummers". They would come up to the orphanage and have masks on and frighten us. I longed to go home, home was only 10 minutes away. Dad was there, also my two brothers Larry and James. Dad could have got some woman in to do the washing and look after us. Our three aunts and grandmother just lived up the road but wouldn't help. I felt desperate. I cried a lot, but it didn't help. Lots of the children cried. I was one among many.

The War was still on. Sister Gabriel would come to the dining hall at teatime, a cup of cocoa and two slices of bread and dripping. Sister Gabriel would read the paper and tell us what was going on. England could have been a million miles

St Joseph's dormitory

away, and about Hitler and the Jews being sent to labour camps. All we could do was pray for these poor people.

When we first went in the orphanage, they'd wait a few months before your guardians swore you in and then if your guardian was of the same view they would take you to the court house. Dad had to swear us in and sign the agreement that us three girls couldn't be taken out until we were 16.

Dad was paying Sarah O'Malley to help him out with Larry and James, brush their hair, wash their clothes, whatever had to be done. She was a fat Scottish woman with eight children of her own. The officials could see that my two brothers were well looked after but they knew there was no way Dad was going to be able to look after us three girls or pay for someone to look after us, they said *"Right, well we're going to draw up this agreement. Now, you swear those kids in until they are 16 and that means that you can't get them out until they're 16"*. You can't sign any papers to get them out or anything like that; they're sworn in and that's the Court ruling and you did that.

I never knew that we were going to be sworn in. It was one day, we were all dressed up and Dad came and got us in the morning and took us to the court house. The officials, like judges, were sitting on the bench and they asked Dad all about why he couldn't look after us and that they had good reports that the two boys were well looked after so perhaps you can look after the girls but Dad said *"No, I can't look after them"*, so they said *"Right"* and then he put the paper in front of Dad and Dad signed it and we all just walked out.

I didn't know anything about being sworn in until Nan

O'Malley told me years later that she went to the orphanage and asked if she could have me because I had turned 16 and they said *"Yeah, we'd give her to you straight away except that we've had a letter from her father to say he's coming over from England for her"*. If we never had the letter, I would have been released to Nan O'Malley and my life would have been totally different, but I'm glad it wasn't because I've got you three kids.

Another year began – 1943. We had jobs to do after school like weeding in one of the many gardens. My job was cleaning one of the school-rooms. I took pride in making the room sparkle and I didn't have to ever be told off about not cleaning up properly. I looked forward to summer.

On 1st May 1943 we went into summer-wear; two summer dresses. We wore the dress for one week then changed, and sent the other dress to be washed. Margo was looked after by a nun and a young girl. Babies got fed different times to us. Margo was too young to know what was happening.

In summertime, the children that had anyone belonging to them like from Achill Island or Castlebar or wherever they came from, maybe an aunt or something, used to send some money to the convent and ask if the children could be bussed to them. So, quite a lot of them used to go actually but there might have been about 40 of us who didn't go on holidays.

What happened was, in the morning (say about ten o'clock) the matron would say *"Right, we're going out to the Sacred Heart School today"* and then she'd open the gate and let us all in and then we'd stay there until twelve o'clock and we were brought in for lunch and then again out to the

Sacred Heart School until about five o'clock. We made our own fun, we played hide and seek because there were lots of trees and green fields and we loved the deer park.

The Convent owned quite a few acres in the country and every year we would be sent to gather in the hay, roll it up into small balls and leave it to dry. A week or so later, we collected the dried hay which was made into haystacks. We had some fun then because as the haystack got bigger, we would rush into it, carrying a bundle of dried stuff and fall down and get covered.

John Malone, the odd job man, didn't think much of our antics, but it made us happy. Bread and jam and milk were had for lunch and when we got back to the orphanage, Mother Alphonsus gave out bonbons to the children who helped most. I never missed out. They were the good times.

Tom Navin with orphans

In summer, mid 1943, I had been sent out on a message to McGreevy's. It was in Westport and obviously the orphanage was in Westport so a lot of the shopkeepers knew me. Mrs McGreevy said *"Oh, wait on a minute Maureen, I've got something for you"* and she came out with this lovely little doll's weighing scales. And I said *"Oh, that's lovely"* because that would be something to play with. So, I went back and the next day I took it out to the Sacred Heart School and we were playing with the scales, we were having a bit of sand on one side and a stone on the other side to see which was heavier and there were a few of us around, and all of a sudden Sister Elizabeth appeared and came over to see what we were all gathered around and she said *"Oh, who gave you that?"* and I said *"Mrs McGreevy"* and she said *"Right"* and the next thing I knew, she'd taken it off us and off she went.

We were playing with the scales on the left of the path. To the right, behind the gate, the nuns kept chickens and once a year a Feis would take place in the green field, a stage would be put up. One year, Kitty got a silver medal for singing, but she lost it down the toilet. The Sacred Heart School is in the background.

My Aunt Annie used to work for Mrs Hockshaw. Mrs Hockshaw lived on Bridge Street and she had a lovely house. She had a shop downstairs where Aunt Annie did everything, she was the cook, the cleaner and there was another guy with her (Mike O'Malley, who she eventually married). One day, in November 1943, Kit and I knocked at the door because we knew Aunt Annie worked for Mrs Hockshaw and we knew that there'd be something there for us maybe a cup of tea and cake.

We had asked Mother Genevieve (a saintly Nun) *"Would it be all right if we went out today?"* and she said *"Yes, yes but you can't take Margo because she's too little"*. So, we knocked at the door and Annie didn't say *"Oh come in"* or anything like that. She said *"What are you two doing here?"* and we said *"We've been let out for the afternoon and we just thought we'd come and see you"*. Now, she mightn't have let us in, but Mrs Hockshaw heard us and she said *"Annie, who's that?"* and she said *"My two nieces, Mrs Hockshaw"*. Mrs Hockshaw said *"Bring them up"*.

So we went up and she was way in the corner in the bedroom; a tiny woman in a nice big bed. And Kit and I looked at each other, you know *"What's going to happen here?"* and she was very interested in Kit and I and asked us who was teaching us, she knew all the nuns. We liked talking to her, and then she said *"Anne, take these children downstairs and make them a nice cup of tea and some cake"* (because Anne used to make cake). Anyway, she said *"Yes, okay, thank you Mrs Hockshaw"* and we said goodbye to her and we went downstairs.

Annie made the cup of tea and she did actually get us the cake and it was all on the table for Kit and me to eat. And then she came back and she put one hand on the back of Kit's chair and one hand on the back of my chair and she said *"Now, I'm going to tell you two something. Your Mother was a tinker"* (and we knew what *tinkers* were) *"and your Father married beneath him"*. I can even see it now; Kit and I looked at each other, we had tears in our eyes and we didn't know what to do and we probably took a drop of tea but left the cake (because we wouldn't have eaten it). What can you say to someone who is a great big woman in her kitchen? We said *"Oh, thank you very much Auntie Anne"* and we just left and went off somewhere else. And I've remembered that forever. It's always there; I can see it like it was yesterday.

In 1974 when Don and I went to see Aunt Annie in hospital in Westport, she asked me where we were going next. I said Ballina. She pulled me right down near her and said *"Whatever you do, don't go to Ballina; they're all drunkards and you'll lose your husband"*. Ballina was where my mother's people came from.

I made friends with a girl called Sarah Doyle. We were together all the time. We loved one another. Sarah used to work in the garden and she would often bring me an apple. Having a friend somehow made up for being in this place. The older girls were always separating us.

I have previously mentioned my friend Bridie Swift who just lived across the road. We've already mentioned my brother Larry going over there, looking up Mrs Swift's clothes. When we went into the orphanage, I was very homesick; in fact, if there was any way of killing myself I would. I remember thinking to myself *"I just don't want to be here and I don't know which is the best way out"*. I do remember that so vividly and just cried myself to sleep every night. When we got out to play in the Industrial School yard, I used to wait for my chance to go down to the other part of the playground and I'd just ask my friend Bridie Swift *"Please Bridie can you go over and ask my Dad to come up and get us because we're very sad and we don't want to be in this place"* and she says *"Yes"*. I used to ask

Westport Courthouse

her just about every day and when I'd see her, she used to say *"Maureen, I go over every day after school when you've asked me, I'd go over and your Dad doesn't say anything; he doesn't say anything, he doesn't say that he is going to pick you up or anything like that"* she said. But I never gave up because I thought the more that you asked him, the more that he would get us out but he never did. And, unbeknownst to me at the time, he couldn't take us home anyway because we were sworn in until we were 16.

When we first went into the orphanage, Dad used to come up every Sunday and collect us (and that was lovely) but after a while, one Sunday, he didn't come up anymore. And so we asked Mother Genevieve if we could go out and see Dad because he hadn't been up to see us. So, she said *"Yes, yes, you can go out"* so Kit and I went up (Margo wasn't allowed because she was too young) and we went up, walked up High Street, The front door was open (nobody ever locked their doors then) and we walked in and couldn't find him and walked all through the house and then we went upstairs (because the little room was right up at the top of the stairs). We walked upstairs and opened the door of that little room and Dad had got a put you up bed there and he was fast asleep, asleep in the bed in the little room. We woke him up. And he said (and I hate to say it but I'm saying it in a good way) *"Jesus, Mary and Joseph. Where have you come from?"* I said *"We've come out to see you Dad, 'cos you didn't come up to see us"*. He said *"Oh, okay then. Give me a minute and I'll get up"*, so we went downstairs and he probably took us up the road. He used to take us up to Tom Carroll's. He might have been out drinking the night before and forgot all about us.

One day when I was out in the town on an errand. I was on my way back to the orphanage and there was a horse in the middle of the road. I mean, horses were around there all the time. Anyway, I looked up at the rider (he was only a young fella, about a year older than me) and I thought to myself *"I know him"* and he said *"Hello"* to me. So, I said *"hello"* and he says *"You're Maureen Noone?"* and I said *"Yeah, I am"* and I said *"Oh, you're John Casey"*. He said *"That's right, from Ardnaree. Yeah, we used to go to Cealtra"*. (This is not the same John Casey who married my Aunt Mamie.) He was from Ardnaree. My Nan lived at 60 Healy Terrace and I would say this John Casey lived at about 70-something. I don't know if Mrs Casey ever went to Cealtra with us, but John did, and that's how he knew me. He got off the horse and he said *"How is it?"* and I said *"Oh, well, Mammy died and we're put in there"* and I don't know what else we talked about. Yeah, he just wanted to know what it was like. I said *"Is everything all right?"* and he said *"Yeah, yeah, we're okay – we're still in the same place and everything"*. John would have ridden his horse from Ballina to Westport.

We loved when Christmastime came along because the stage went up and we couldn't wait for Christmas dinner because we'd get a really nice dinner with a little bit of meat and gravy. We loved peas but we never got peas, so peas on Christmas Day was lovely and then Sister Vincent would come around with custard and jelly. That made our day. And then after that, we'd go down into the school and we all sat around and everybody got the rag doll present. When I got to be about 14, I was one of the people that when everyone went to bed at night, they'd call out your name and they'd say *"We're making dolls tonight for the young ones"*. But by the time you were fourteen, if you wore socks up to your knees, you got a lovely pair of long black stockings and you got garters and then you were grown-up and you'd look at yourself in the mirror and you'd think *"Oh, this is lovely"*.

We used to be taken for walks to the Quay. In winter, you know if the day was cold, we'd all get dressed up in black coats and black berets and two nuns would come with us always, they'd be at the back. I wasn't one of those girls that used to keep order at that time because I was only little, but when you

The fields where we played during the summer holidays.

get to be about eleven and twelve, then you get your own, say, seven or eight children and you are responsible for everything they do, how they're dressed, if there's holes in their socks. Every Wednesday when they changed their underwear, if that's lost, then on the Wednesday they haven't got a pair of pants to put on, you've got to go up to the drying room and you could be there all night looking for these and then eventually they'll give you a new pair of pants if you can't find the old ones and I don't know what happened to them.

To get back to the walks, the two nuns used to follow us and depending on what nuns they were, we knew what we could get away with. So, if it was Sister Magdalene, she was English and we were happy. After lunch we would line up and off we'd go. We loved the country walks seeing all the lambs and horses and we would pick haws from the hawthorn tree and eat them. They were red berries, floury but not much taste.

At different times we'd go out. One of the good times is if we were all going out to the Quay, when we went by Glenn's. They were iron mongers and they were on Shop Street. We were called the *"Black Army"* because we were always dressed in black and black caps on us, so people used to say *"Oh, the Black Army has just gone by"* but Mr Glenn would always come outside his door when we were walking past his shop and he would wait to see me, especially, because I was the oldest of the Noones and then he'd put sixpence in my hand and he'd say go and get an icecream. This happened a lot. Any time we ever went past the shop and he'd see us, he always gave us, not a lot of money but enough to buy an ice cream at McHales.

But one day we went out to the Quay and we were caught in a real storm. One of the girls there was actually from the Quay (her name was Madge Moran) and she had lived in the cottage at the Quay but her mother had died but she had an aunt there and she said *"I'll just run across the road and see if it's all right for us all to go over and shelter ..."* – I mean, there was about four cottages there with a lovely shelter over them. She came back and she said *"Yeah, we can all go over"* so we went over and we're standing there and one of the doors opened and a guy came out, a young fella. I was 13 at the time; he probably would have been about 17. So he said *"Oh God, you all look soaked"* and we said *"yeah"* so he brought some towels out but there were so many kids. By the time you got the towel it was wet anyway.

He said *'So, how is it in there then? Tell us what happens in there? What do you get up to?"* and I said *"Well, most mornings we get bread and dripping and a cup of tea; but at lunchtime we get a bowl of porridge and maybe a cup of cocoa. At 3 o'clock we get (again) two slices of bread and dripping and sometimes the dripping that you get out of when you fry lamb chops* (but we never saw the lamb chops; that's probably from the nuns' lamb chops, but not from ours) *and then what we used to do, when nobody was looking, we'd squeeze the bread together and the dripping would go on the floor and then we'd get rid of it under the table and eat the dry bread. For teatime, we'd get the same. And next day would be a little bit different because lunchtime there'd be meatballs. But soup (with things floating on top – which we never realised what they were ... but they were probably all right 'cos nobody died)"* and if there was a good orphanage we were in it. This fella said *"Are they alright to youse in there?"* and I said *"yes but there's one, Sister Elizabeth, and we don't like her."* He said *"You tell Sister Elizabeth to come and see me and leave her knickers off."* I didn't know how to answer this. I knew he was implying something dirty but I didn't know what it was.

I don't know why Madge was in the orphanage because her aunt was living in the cottages at the Quay. Madge was a lovely singer and shortly after Kit, Margo and I went into the orphanage, Madge left. But a couple of years after that, she arrived back and there was great excitement because we asked her to sing and she was singing all the songs from, say, 1944-45 like all the War songs and all that. So, on Sunday afternoons we'd get a lovely lot of the kids together and Madge sang all the songs for us and she was dressed lovely and she had lipstick on and we were all thinking *"How lovely it will be when one day we'll get out of here, we'll have nice clothes and be happy."*

When I was eleven (in 1944) all the orphans got 'the itch'. Every morning the 76 of us would walk in our night dresses into a little room. Behind a curtain was Mother Ursula and Kathleen Corcoran. They had a bucket full of white water and a 5 inch paint brush. One by one we would go behind the curtain, take off our night dress and they would paint us all over with this white stuff which I think was lime. Then we would put our nightdress back on and go back to bed. This happened every day for a week. The nuns brought up our meals to us in bed and none of us went to school.

I remember writing the date 4-4-44 in my exercise book. Just before school that morning, we were giving our shoes a rub. One of the girls mentioned we would be writing for 4-4-44 in our books today. I remember that as well as though it was yesterday.

We were well in the orphanage when one day we came out to see Dad. He said *"I've got something to show you"*. He said *"Turn that button there"* and I turned it on and light came on. Dad had got electric light. I had seen electricity already in other peoples' houses that Mammy used to clean and we had electric light in the orphanage so I was pleased he had it, no more oil lamps.

Sister Magdalene was a nice nun. When she would turn her back to the class to write something on the board, Kit would get out on the floor and make us laugh, kicking her heels up. Sister Magdalene would turn around and ask *"What are you all laughing at?"* and Mary Grimes would say *"Kitty Noone is making us laugh"*. One day Sister Magdalene had had enough and when Mary Grimes said *"Kitty Noone is making us laugh"* Sister Magdalene said *"Kitty Noone is one of the brightest girls in the class"* and she sent Mary Grimes out of the room. Kit got away with a lot.

In the summer, if we were going somewhere where we could swim we'd all get a calico swimsuit. You can imagine, when calico is wet, it sticks to you and when you get to be like about twelve or thirteen, you're getting boobs and downstairs and all that, you know, so you don't want anybody seeing you. The first time they gave it to us, we all went in the water and we were happy, after that, we'd say *"No, no, we don't want to swim"* so we never learnt to swim because we were too embarrassed to wear the things.

There was me and Angela McCormick and Agnes Quinn (I don't know who the other girl was) but there was four of us and we all wanted to do a wee in the middle of the night. And of course there's 76 of us in this dormitory, we had no light. I'm all skittish about what could be around, so we're walking down in between the beds to go way down to the other end to the toilet and Angela McCormick said *"Oh, what's that?"* and Agnes Quinn said *"What?"* and she said *"Oh, something is round here somewhere"*, so us four started screaming and screaming and everyone was awake in the dormitory.

Catherine Corcoran made our dresses and habits for the nuns. She came out with the Matron and they turned the light on and said *"What's wrong?"* and I said *"We were going to the toilet and Angela McCormick saw something and she was really scared"*. Well, all the nuns heard us in the convent and a whole lot of them came out and the next day, Sister

Stanislaus said (because Agnes Quinn didn't know much; she was like Sadie Doyle, not very bright. Not so much simple, just that she couldn't learn things, so she wasn't in favour. You're only in favour really if you were smart. So, she was going to get the brunt of it and she was the oldest as well) so Sister Stanislaus said *"We're all going to write a story about the ghost in the dormitory"*.

She told the story and said what our names were and we had to write it in our composition books. It's down forever there and we're all looking at each other and every time she mentioned our name, she'd say *"And Maureen Noone! We thought that she was a bit smart but – not"*. And *"Angela McCormick, you should have something going for you. I mean you're out there and you're intelligent"... "We're having a nice sleep and everybody is happy and then four nutcases got up to go to the toilet and woke everybody up!"* And of course the nuns were all out, all over the place, wondering if someone had got into the dormitory, probably killed us or something. So yeah, we're writing it; she's telling us what to write and we are all copying it down. It was a good story.

There was an old man called Crow Carroll. That was just a nickname for him. He was a big man and he had another guy staying there with him and this other guy was a pensioner. We went in to see Crow Carroll. Dad was there and this old guy was asking us all about the orphanage and we said we didn't like it much and we'd love to come out and live with Dad and he put his hand in his pocket and he said *"I just got my pension this morning"* and I didn't know how much he gave us. Later I counted it and it was eight shillings (in two shilling pieces) and I said *"Look what Mr so-and-so has given us"* and Dad said *"Oh, that's good"* and I thought *"Shall I give it to Dad?"* and I thought at the time *"We'll keep it because we never get any money or have anything"*. Dad knew I had eight shillings but he didn't have the gall to ask me for it. I was on the verge of giving it to him but I didn't.

So we went into the convent and I gave it up (because I had to give it up). I gave it up to the Matron, Kathleen Corcoran. When we used to go out for a walk on Sunday, she'd give me some of it and then I'd go into McHale's Ice Cream place and I'd buy icecream for a few friends.

I went out again on a message and I don't know who gave me one shilling and three pennies. I went back to the orphanage and never said anything to anyone, kept the *"one and three"* as we used to say and the next time I was sent out on a message, I went into a chemist and I was looking at all the things in the chemist. I saw some clear nail varnish and I thought *"Oh, I'd love to get some of that"*. I thought *"I'll have that"*. So I gave him the *"one and three"* and I took the nail varnish.

I went back to the orphanage. I had a friend, Teresa, and I said to her *"I've got something on, but it's got to be like a real secret. It's nail varnish and you put it on your nails. You can't see it, but it will be lovely and shiny"*. So we both went into a huddle in the toilet (where nobody else could come in) and I put mine on first and then I did hers. And we walked out of there and we met Jojo Canavan. It's like it was yesterday; I can see Jojo, and Teresa says *"Look at my nails"*. So, Jojo says *"Oh, how did you get your nails so shiny?" "I'll tell you what, go up to the dormitory and find the wax and keep on putting the wax on your nails* (this is Teresa) *and in the end, it will turn out like this".* So, Jojo went up to the dormitory, got the tin of wax that we used to polish the floors with every Saturday, came down, her fingers were full of wax and Teresa said *"You're not doing it properly".* Jojo said *"Oh what are you rubbing it in with?"* and she said *"Oh, a bit of paper. You'd better go and get a hankie or something like that".* Anyway, Jojo came back about an hour or so later and she said *"Look, I nearly scrubbed my nails off. It's still not doing it".* And Teresa said *"Oh, don't worry. It will shine later, it takes time".*

One of my jobs was to carry coal and turf for the fires. Sister Elizabeth was in charge of lighting the fires. I remember once I carried a bucket of turf to Saint Ursula's room. It had been snowing and I had done my best to pick dry turf. Sister Elizabeth said she would come with me next day and show me where the dry turf was. The snow covered much of the stack. I went to put a small piece in the bucket, only to have Sister Elizabeth bang me over my hand with a bigger piece of turf. Obviously I wasn't doing the job right.

I had a little box that I used to put under my bed and I had holy pictures and a little bit of soap that had a nice smell. One morning, the same Sister Elizabeth, came into the dormitory and for some reason or other this morning, she looked under my bed and found the little box with my bits and pieces in it and took it down and gave it to Mother Ursula. Mother Ursula was the one who had a great big long, thick leather strap. It was about eight inches long and an inch and a half thick and it had a long sort of a strap on the end so that when she hit you, she could really give you a good old whack.

So, I was out at the Sacred Heart School (it was my turn to look after the kids in the summer) and Katey Bolingbrook (a great friend of mine) came out and said *"Mother Ursula wants to see you"* and I said *"Why?"* I knew that I was doing everything all right. She said *"Oh, I don't know but she wants to see you"*. I thought *"Okay"*. I said *"Can you look after the gate? Don't let anybody in or out until I come back"*.

So, I went in to Mother Ursula and she had the box on the table. I thought *"Oh my nail varnish is in there"*. She asked *"Is this your box?"* and I said *"Yes it is, Mother"* and she said *"Well, I'm going to open it because there's something in it that I'm not very happy about"*. I knew what it was and I thought *"Oh"* and so she opened it up and she said *"Where did you get this?"* So I said *"When I went out on Sunday to see my cousin, she gave it to me"*. And she said *"Well, next time you see your cousin you tell her to take the dirt out from under her nails and not to give you anything like this again"* and she gave it to Kathleen Corcoran. She said *"You might be able to use it"*. Gave me back my box of pictures and she said *"And now* (and she's taking this thing out ...) *hold your hands out"* and I did, and she walloped me on the hands with the strap. She hit me four times, but I mean it was a big leather strap. I'd be twelve, going on thirteen then. I told her that a cousin gave it to me because if I told her that I went out and bought it at the chemist shop she would have put me in the book as *"Don't send Maureen Noone out on any more messages because she's going into chemists and buying stuff"*.

I've explained how the first four classes used to have their bath one Wednesday and the next four classes used to have their bath the following Wednesday, so you waited a fortnight for a bath. There was a lovely enclosed bathroom upstairs just for nuns. They had their own bathroom in the convent, but when the kids weren't having a bath, Sister Elizabeth, Mother Evangelist (who was lovely) and Mother Ursula, they would use this bathroom that was out in the orphanage. Mother Ursula used to go up there on a Wednesday afternoon and come down looking good. Kathleen Corcoran used to go up with her because she was so dumpy she could hardly get around so Kathleen Corcoran used to bring her up all those stairs up to the dressing room and then bring her into the bathroom. I always knew when she had a shower because her face was, you know, lovely and clean. She used to change her clothes and all that stuff around her head. But anyway, that was her. But it's funny, I would never have remembered that if I hadn't been talking about something else.

As I would turn twelve in the December (1944) I was given more jobs. One of my jobs was to get up at 2.00 am every morning for one week and call the babies and young children who wet the bed. I would take them one by one to the toilet, see they went to the toilet and take them back to bed. In the middle of winter it was hard going; I would be freezing and the poor children would be the same, but that was the rule, otherwise there would be wet beds. The sheets would have to go to the laundry and in wet weather they took ages to dry. The laundry was run by women who had grown up in the orphanage. No one claimed them and they ended up working in the laundry for five shillings a week and some would stay there until they were old and died.

One morning after I had checked to see none of the children had wet the bed, I checked on one of the new children, Mary B was her name, to take her to the toilet. I found she was lying on a bed of worms, (later she got medicine and was fixed). I went back to my bed. As I had been up in the night, I was allowed to lie in. Sister Elizabeth came through at 6.00 am, threw back the bedclothes of all the young ones, found that Annette Gawley had been sick, came over to my bed and ordered me out to the dressing room. There, Sister Elizabeth took a wooden-backed hairbrush and began hitting me. I crouched down but she still hit me. Same morning, 11.30 am, Mother Evangelist took us for Catechism. I told Mother Evangelist what had happened and within two weeks Sister Elizabeth wasn't in charge anymore and we got lovely Sister Anne. Sister Elizabeth got Sister Anne's job wheeling a nun around in a wheelchair at the convent.

About this time (I was twelve and a half years old) I scratched my leg with a rusty needle. The way that happened was, study began every night at 5.00 pm. I was late this night, it was raining and I had my overall on. I kept a needle in one of the folds. My legs were wet so I wiped my legs and scratched my right leg below the knee. The needle was rusty, so after a few days my knee was really sore. I showed it to the matron. She said I should rest it. I stayed in bed next day; the doctor had a look at it. I was having poultices on it; my knee was getting bigger every day. I was still in bed with it, then one day my knee just burst open and pus and blood started coming out of it. I was frightened. The dormitory was locked every day and I was locked in there on my own. I got out of bed, stood on the toilet and looked out. The children were playing so it took me some time to get attention. Later, Mother Ursula came up and saw to my knee. It was a mess. Dr McGing had a look at it and said I would have to stay in bed for a few days and have it dressed. I remember it being very sore and feeling a bit weak when I did get up but looking back now, after all these years, I could have lost my leg, so I thank God everything turned out fine.

Dad would come to the orphanage from time to time and take us out for the day. We would go for a walk or Dad would take us to see Gran. She seemed pleased to see us. Aunt Katie and Aunt Annie lived with Gran at that time. We would have a cup of tea and some Irish bread and before we knew it, time was up and we were back behind bars again.

One day I came out to do some messages. Baby Giblin shouted my name *"Maureen!"* and I looked around and I said *"Oh Baby. I haven't seen you for a long time"*. She said *"No, I've been in hospital"*. I found out later on that she'd been in a mental institution, so that explained why she was yelling and screaming in the middle of the night and waking us all up, poor lady when we lived next door to her in High Street.

The War was still on. Southern Ireland didn't know too much about it. We didn't have to have lights out in case we were bombed. Hitler called us a "*cabbage garden*" and wouldn't be bothered with us. Sister Gabriel was still reading us bits from the paper. Can you imagine 76 young children eating bread and dripping and worrying about what was happening in

England? However, in May 1945, Sister Gabriel came to the dining room and with great gusto announced the War was over. We thought *"What does this mean? Do we get butter now? Maybe the occasional egg?"* because, so far, eggs were only for the children who looked ill. Seeing that I was always looking well, eggs were something I only got on Easter Sunday.

About this time, I started to look at myself, not yet thirteen years. I'd look in the mirror and think *"I don't look too bad*". I started to take care of myself. School Certificate was on the cards. I wanted to pass because if I didn't, I could end up being a servant girl and I wanted to do something with my life.

In June 1945, Mum's half-sister, Mamie McDermott, now married to John Casey, wrote to the orphanage and asked if Kitty and I could go on holiday to Ballina. She sent the fare, five shillings. The nuns allowed us to go. Poor Margo didn't go, she was too young. We got on the bus in Westport. When the bus got to Ballina, there wasn't anyone there to pick us up. I remembered where Ardnaree was because we used to go on holidays to see Nan, so we went in that direction. I asked someone where 24 Bunree Road was. Aunt Mamie had gone for messages but one of the neighbours called out to her and she came running back. Number 24 was a cottage, no bathroom, but a big sink. John Casey was a lovely man.

I asked Aunt Mamie where Nan was. I was shocked and terribly sad when she told me Nan had died in 1944 of a broken heart, because Mammy had died.

James McDermott was still alive and Mamie was really scared of him. We were walking one day and she saw him on the bridge. She said *"Oh, there's my Dad on the bridge"*. She said *"We'll have to go another way"* so instead of crossing the bridge we had to go the long way round, past St Murdach's Cathedral. After Nan died, Mamie moved and something happened, maybe it was that she left her Dad on his own, John had gone to England so maybe he thought Mamie should look after him.

Uncle Johnnie McDermott was Aunt Mamie's brother. He was a very good-looking man and he also lived at number 24. John Casey moved upstairs and left Kit and I the bed with Aunt Mamie downstairs. This was to prove the best holiday we ever had. We made friends with young kids around the place, Tommy Ginty, Harry Murray, Larry Holmes, Annie Kate McLoughlin and her sister, Sheila. Caught up with all our old friends.

That summer, we raided orchards. Tommy asked me if I would like a roll. I said *"yes"*. So we all went to this field. Tommy lay down on the grass. He said for me to lie on top of him and then we proceeded to roll down the hill, over and over again. It felt great; I didn't know why I felt so good and we did it again. What would the nuns have said if they knew?

Aunt Mamie was lovely to us. Her husband John Casey didn't say much. All too soon it was time to go back to the orphanage. We would have given anything to stay in Ballina but that wasn't possible. After all, Dad had sworn us in. So that's where we had to stay, reason being that Dad couldn't keep taking us out and putting us back when we became too much for him to look after us. Otherwise, we wouldn't know where we belonged. Looking back, I'm sure I would have coped.

My thirteenth birthday was looming. Now it was my turn to look after seven children. I tried to be kind to the children under my care. I was scarcely a child myself. My job was to see that none of the seven children I looked after had holes in their socks, that they were dressed properly. I was also responsible to see that the children washed their teeth and brushed their hair. I learned very early in life what motherhood was all about. All my children had grey flannel dresses and petticoats, except for Teresa who had a jumper and skirt. I didn't know the reason then but I found out later that Teresa's mother paid five shillings a week for her.

The nuns would have a look at you and see if you were *"compassionate"* or what sort of a person you were and then when anything happened and there were sick children in the infirmary (because that's what we used to call it) then they'd put you on the list to tend to the sick. My name was put on the list when I was fourteen. It was a great job because the infirmary had a fireplace. There wouldn't only be me in there; there was Biddy Hancock (Biddy was about 6 foot tall) and she eventually ended up being a nun, but Mary Hancock (her sister) was in the kitchen and that was long before I got my job in the kitchen. Sadie Doyle and Biddy Hancock were on duty with me when May Garvey was brought in very ill. May was as deaf as a post. She couldn't hear anything.

Not only was May brought in, but a little girl was brought in. Moggy Gawley was her name. Moggy Gawley was about two. Mary, Moggy and Annette was the youngest. Moggy was a beautiful, red-haired baby. At the time, nobody knew what was wrong with her but she started to swell up. Sister Vincent had a great heart (I had a lot of time for Sister Vincent). She would go and sit on Moggy's bed and she'd have a little bit of mashed potatoes or custard or something like that and she'd feed it to Moggy and Moggy would spit it out because she just didn't want it, she was too ill. And Sister Vincent used to be very sad about this and tried her hardest, making Moggy eat it and it used to worry us because we knew that Moggy was so ill. Anyway, Moggy died. And so that was sad because we were looking after her and you'd think there would have been something that we could have done but obviously not.

May Garvey, while we were there, died as well (she was quite old). I suppose she would have been about 40 which would have seemed old to me at the time. She worked with Sister Gabriel. Sister Gabriel was the nun that was coming down to the dining hall, you know, we called it that. I don't know what they used to call it. But it was three big long tables in this dining hall and on the first table was all the babies and all the young people and on the second table there used to be, say, about five on one side, five on the other side and they were the ones that were poorly and needed the eggs at the top of the table (like I said before) so they didn't have to go all around the dining room; they used to just put the egg in front of them at the table. As I say we got one Easter Sunday but these kids that were poorly got one maybe a couple of times a week.

One day in 1946 I had to run an errand for one of the nuns

and as I was running along Mill Street, the thought came to me *"I'd love to see my Dad"*, so I ran up High Street. Dad was sitting in his workshop. He would mostly mend shoes but if anyone wanted shoes made to measure, he would make them. He was very proud of himself as he showed me the shoes he had made. He said *"Look at these"*. And if you went into a shoe shop, that's what you would expect to find. Dad didn't make our shoes but he mended them. We didn't go without shoes while he was there. He gave me tuppence for an ice-cream. I took off, did the message, and tore back to school. That happened a lot after that. Every time I was sent on a message, I would go and see Dad. Sometimes Dad would call for us on a Sunday and take us out for a walk and home to our old house we grew up in. We were always sad when we had to go back to the orphanage.

In June 1946, I was about to sit my School Certificate but just before I sat for this exam, Sister Stanislaus thought I wasn't prepared enough and wouldn't let me sit the exam. I was sad about it, but I knuckled down and thought, "*There's always next year*".

CHAPTER FIVE

1946 - 1949
Dad Leaves For London

In summer 1946 Dad came to see us and told us he was going to England. Larry and James were to be put in a home in Galway. I thought *"Well, that's that. I'll rot in this place"*. I asked Dad when he was going to England. He told me the 8.00 am train from Westport to Dublin. I asked permission from the nuns to go to the train station. Obviously, Dad never expected me. Dad was standing on the platform waiting for his train and Mrs O'Malley was a little further away. This was the Scottish woman with a husband and six kids of her own who Dad had been paying to help him look after Larry and James. I said "*What's Mrs O'Malley doing here?*" Dad said "*I suppose she's off to Scotland*". I was suspicious. I found out years later from Sarah herself that she was pregnant to my Dad at that time and that's why they had to leave Westport.

After he got to London, Dad sometimes sent us five shillings.

I was studying hard. I must get that School Certificate. About this time, we went to visit Dad's sisters, Aunt Kate and Annie. (Aunt Beazie was married to Mac McCarthy and still lived in the next house but one). Katie said "*I think your*

This is a photograph of Sister Elizabeth, the Nun about whom I have the most bad memories.

father should know, Martin has married again". Katie said the new wife was fat. She made me sit down and write to Dad and say "*Martin has married a hay bag*". (Martin was Dad's brother). As I wrote the letter I remembered the time Aunt Annie told Kit and me that my Mammy was a tinker and that my Dad married beneath him. The Noones were good at running other people down, but being as Kitty and I had no one, we had to grin and bear it.

We found Kate more funny after Dad went to England. Even though Kit and I didn't want to have anything to do with them because they weren't good to Mammy, they were all we had. When we'd come out on the Sunday, Kate used to make us laugh from start to finish and everything was good in that house until Auntie Anne arrived, after finishing work at Hockshaws. The minute Anne came in, everything changed. She wasn't funny. Us kids didn't say anything because we knew *"Aunt Anne is coming"*. Granny used to say to Kate when we'd arrive: *"Kate, Kate, who do these children belong to?"* and Kate said *"Jim, and he's in London and they're in the convent"*. Gran would ask the same question several times. She would only have been in her fifties at this time.

In 1947 I sat my School Certificate. As I entered the school to take my place, I was shaking like a jellyfish. Sister Stanislaus said to me *"It's no use shaking now. If you have studied well, you've got nothing to worry about"*. Bridget O'Toole sat along from me. I looked pleadingly at her. She was great at fractions and mental arithmetic and a couple of times during the exam, she told me the answers to a couple of sums. Thank God we were not caught as my Certificate wouldn't be hanging on the wall now.

When the results were read out and my name was called, I was so happy. Everyone who passed got an ice-cream. That ice cream tasted great and now that I had passed my School Certificate, I was allowed to learn book-keeping. I went on to the sixth class and sometimes was asked to take a class of slow readers.

I would turn fifteen in December 1947. I remember seeing magazines from England of Princess Elizabeth and her husband Philip. I thought how marvellous to be a real live princess getting married. I only ever read about this happening in my story book. I would only read stories that began with "*Once upon a time*" because I knew the story ended with the line "*They lived happily ever after*".

I remember 1948 as being a good year. Having passed my

This photo of the nuns would have been taken in the 1940's. The Nuns are, left to right;
Sister Collett and Sister Juliana were sisters in real life. They cooked for the other nuns. Sister Stanislaus would hit my head against the blackboard when I didn't or couldn't do my sums. Sister Mary Mercy taught me in Standard One. Sister Columba taught me in Standard Two; she was a lovely nun. Sister Lewis taught me in Standard Three in 1942 (?); She often hit me. Sister Gertrude taught me in Standard Four from September 1942;

I liked her. Sister Stanislaus taught me in Standard Five. Sister Kevin took us for cooking; she was a grouch.

I liked Sister Ann who looked after the children when Sister Elizabeth was taken off the job.

I complained to Mother Evangelist, pictured in the middle of the photograph with glasses, about how Sister Elizabeth had beaten me so much with a wooden hairbrush, I couldn't stand up. Sister Malaka was a bit eccentric; She's the nun who was looking away from the camera.

School Certificate in 1947, Sister Gertrude decided to teach me book-keeping. Also, I was allowed to go to a shorthand class run by Sister Bernadette (the nun who said she would pin my lips together when I was seven. She didn't show any recognition and no smile). I learned the first book in Pitman's Shorthand. I still have this book. There was also a typewriter in the school and I sometimes would try and type, but I never got the hang of it. I kept on with the book-keeping and shorthand and hoped that when December came, and I would turn sixteen years, Dad would come over from England and take me out of the orphanage. It would be sad to leave Kitty and Margo, but that was the way it had to be.

I also learned to make a dress and to knit. I knitted myself a brown jumper, not the colour I would have picked, but the wool was given to me. Surprisingly, I was allowed to wear it. I suppose whoever was in charge of what we should wear decided I'd worn the grey flannels long enough.

One day I was called in to see the Matron, Kathleen Corcoran. She explained to me that I was getting big in the chest area and, from now on, I would have to wear a binder. She measured me and told me the binder would be ready in a few days. I remember putting the binder on. It had hooks and eyes down the left side. It was to keep us looking flat and also stop us from wobbling when we ran. We only had one, so we had to wash it pronto and get it back on. I wondered if the nuns wore one of these things too. I would stand in front of the mirror in the dressing room doing my hair. It was quite straight but I had put a wave in it and I thought "*One day, when I get out of this place, I'll get a perm*".

In the summer of 1948 I was in charge of the children who didn't go on holiday. Somehow, it was a good summer; things were getting better and it would be my last summer in the orphanage and I decided to make the most of it. I suppose you could compare it to a prisoner who had almost served his time. We spent most of the summer holidays out in the Deer Park. We helped with the hay and life was good. I was writing to Dad and saying I hoped he could come in December and take me to England. Just the thought of being free made me so happy.

I also got my period. I went to see Kathleen Corcoran, told her what had happened. She told me I would be getting this all my life. Kathleen gave me five towels. These were mine. I would wear them, wash them, try to dry them as best I could. I thought to myself *"This growing-up business is not too good"*, what with the binder and now this. I didn't know why we got periods; it was all very worrying. I didn't talk to anyone about it and it reminds me of a friend telling me one day she thought she was turning into a monkey. I asked her why. Anna said *"I have hair under my arms and at the top of my legs"*. I said *"So have I, but I think it's supposed to be there"*. Looking back, how innocent we were.

When the December concert came, Kitty and I sang "The Old House". The first lines were:

"Lonely I wander
Through dreams of my childhood
They bring back those memories
Of happy days of yore.

Gone are the old folk
The house stands deserted
No light in the window
No welcome at the door."

We both wore tartan skirts, jumpers and we had lipstick put on by Sister Kevin. All the nuns sat in rows and we thought we were great, coming out on stage, singing. I was also in the play. I was the father, sitting down reading the paper and telling my two sons (who were girls) off because they were boxing. Christmas-time was always a good time and the nuns did appreciate the time and effort we put into learning our lines. My birthday had come and gone but I hadn't heard from Dad. I wondered if he wanted me.

The year 1949 started well. Now that I was 16 years, the nuns decided I should earn some money. It was decided that I should keep up my shorthand and book-keeping, but I was given a job in the kitchen. Sister Vincent was in charge. The morning was taken up with me helping to wash the potatoes and getting them into the boiler to be ready for the children at 12 o'clock. The big cooking range was full of pots, some with mince meatballs, soup and cabbage. At 11.30 am, Sister Vincent, Mary Finn and myself would peel all the potatoes.

Sister Vincent would say *"We'll have to get the eggs out for the kids that are not well"* so I'd get the saucepan out, she'd count the eggs and then just boil them and then she'd go down to the place where we had our meals, in "*the refectory*" I think they used to call it, and she'd come around and just put out a soft-boiled egg for all the people that were poorly.

One of my jobs was to lay out two trays at lunchtime; one

tray was for the old witch Miss O'Shaunessy (dressmaker). The other tray was for Kathleen Corcoran. Kathleen Corcoran used to eat down in the refectory where we used to eat and she'd be over at a table on her own and you'd have to bring her tray down there. She couldn't eat an awful lot of things because she had ulcers in her stomach and every now and then she would have to go away to the hospital.

The children would file into the dining room, Grace was said and then silence. If you spoke, you were made to stand up all through the meal. I had been through all that. Now I was working, I ate my lunch when everyone else had finished. I must say, I did love working in the kitchen. I watched the bread boy deliver the bread and thought how nice-looking he was. My job was to cut the bread, put the dripping on, or sometimes (believe it or not) the children got butter or jam.

I would be in the storeroom on my own. I would ladle some cream off the milk and drink it. If Katie Bolingbroke, my sisters, Kitty or Margo, or Teresa came to the storeroom door, I would always give them a couple of slices of bread or cream if they wanted it. We had to be quick, as Sister Vincent trusted me.

I was sent on messages to the butchers and loved to get out and feel free. I had moved from the dormitory with 76 beds to a smaller one. Most of the people in the small dormitory were 16 years and over. Some of the older ones were there because, through no fault of theirs, no one came to claim them. They started working like me and time just passed them by. Maggie Burke was the oldest, I'd say about 40. She assumed she was in charge of everyone. There were twins there, Una and Josie Rogers. Una left and got herself a job. You can leave at 16 because you then are no longer a ward of the Court but Josie stayed on, and Maggie and Josie used to have some heated arguments, mostly about what Josie did or did not do in the laundry that day.

I'd lie there and think *"I would never put up with someone always bellyaching at me"*. Josie was years older than me, but her and I got on well, sometimes making faces behind Maggie's back. Granny Grady was another person who just let time pass her by. By now, Granny was getting the pension. She was a kindly soul but she would rattle on about something, usually with Sister Gabriel telling her to be quiet.

One day I was working in the kitchen and Sister Vincent (who was a really nice nun) gave me the keys of the cupboard outside and she said *"I haven't got any time, can you go and open the cupboard and get a pound of butter out of there?"* so I opened the cupboard. I was dumbfounded to see (and I can see it now) my scales on the shelf. These were the scales I was given five years before that were confiscated by Sister Elizabeth. But now I was 16 and I thought *"What am I going to do with them?"* and if I took them, would Sister Vincent know that I had taken them (even though they were mine). So I left them there. But it was just something that stayed with me all my life, to think that Sister Elizabeth took them off me and gave them to Sister Vincent who had no use for them, they were just a toy.

I was glad I was in the kitchen. Apart from the odd piece of toast and butter, I'd make myself other perks. The girls who worked in the laundry never seemed to get a break. I'd wander over sometimes. Sarah Doyle, who was one of my friends, was busy washing on a washing board. All the nuns' clothes were washed in this laundry. All sanitary towels were first put into buckets of cold water, let soak, then washed. When the basket was full, the girls would take them up the hill and lay them out on the grass to get the stains out of them. Washing day was Monday; Wednesday was ironing day. All the headpieces that the nuns wore were starched and ironed. I would duck into the ironing room and watch the girls hard at work.

I was in charge also of going way down to what we used to call *"the pond"*. There was no pond there but it got the name of *"the pond"* and when you went down there, there were great big sheds where the three gardeners and odd job men worked. One of the sheds had anthracite in it and it was my job to fill up this great big container (about a metre high) and it had a lip on it, so we could easily turf the anthracite into the fire. It was my job every day to make sure that there was enough anthracite. I went into the pitch dark shed and was shovelling it up. I used to jam the door a little bit open with a stone because otherwise I would have to feel with my hand to see where the anthracite was. It's like coal but it's very, very little. It's a special kind of coal. One day I was filling up my container and the door opened a little bit wider and it was John Malone and he was standing at the door and he started singing *"I'd love to get you on a slow boat to China"* ... I bet he would because his wife, now she was very fat. They had seven sons and they lived in the gatehouse to the convent on the right as you come in.

Mary Finn, who used to help me peel the potatoes every day for the children's lunch, decided to go into town without telling anyone. Sister Vincent asked me if I knew where Mary was. I said she'd gone into town. Sister Vincent assumed I had something to do with it and she was right. Mary mentioned to me she'd like to see the bread boy. I told her to take herself into town and visit where the one I liked worked, however when Mary came back, she was told off severely and she didn't see her fellow.

Sunday afternoons, all the girls would meet in the kitchen. We would put records on and some would dance. Sarah Doyle was a good dancer and she would show us how to waltz. For the first time in my life, I had a little cupboard where I could store things and no one interfered with anything that was mine. Our dressing room was smaller than the one I was used to before I moved up to being a kitchenhand.

I was getting on well with my shorthand and book-keeping. I wondered if Dad would ever come.

CHAPTER SIX

1949
Leaving The Orphanage

It was coming on towards summer, 1949. I wrote to Dad again saying that I was now able to leave the orphanage and will he come and get me. I had an answer back to say Dad was coming over in June. It was now April and things started to happen. I was given a small case.

Kathleen Corcoran gave me: –

One red jumper that I had knitted.
One black skirt that I had made with help.
One pink blouse that I had made with help.
A summer dress, white with green dots.
One grey pinafore dress.
Two pairs of white ankle socks.
Two knickers.
I asked for another summer dress but
Kathleen Corcoran wouldn't give it to me.

It was around this time that Nan O'Malley went up to the convent to see if she could get me out, to teach me hairdressing. Nan told me about this in 1974 and she also told me that her mother bought the wedding ring for my mother.

Sister Gertrude came to see me one morning and she said *"Maureen, this £30 is for all the time that you've worked in the kitchen. I've opened a Post Office book for you"* and I said *"Oh"* and she said *"You're going to need it when you go to London"*. I said *"Thank you very much"*. I didn't even know that I was going to be paid; no one told me. I just did it because it was a job.

On a bright summer's day in June 1949, Dad arrived at the orphanage. I remember waking up that morning and thinking *"I will be free today"*, but then I thought of Kitty and Margo who were going to be left behind. They would have to wait their turn.

I asked Dad if we could go and see Larry and James. We (Dad, me, Kit and Margo) took a bus to Galway and called at St Joseph's Salthill Industrial School (run by the Christian Brothers). We asked for Larry and James Noone. We all went to a café and had fish and chips. We talked about me going to London and how I would help them, but things didn't turn out as I thought they would.

We took Larry and James back to Salthill. They held hands as they walked down a long corridor. I promised Larry and James that I would come back and get them. But I never did. To this day I feel guilty about that. I will finish this part of my story here. The next part of my story will start the day I arrived in London.

Postscript

In 1951, Dad and I returned to Westport because it was Kit's turn to leave the orphanage. We took some photos. Margo had to stay behind.

Kit and I had three wonderful and mischievous years in London before I left with Don in 1954, for New Zealand. Our plan was to go for two years but, five months after we arrived, Don's parents and brother emigrated to New Zealand. That put paid to all talk of returning home. It was another 20 years before Don and I could afford to return to London, in 1974. Kit arranged for Larry and James to meet us in a pub. Margo came along too of course.

In the 1950's, Kit had discovered Tom was in a mental institution. He was 14 years old. Kit arranged for her husband Bill and our brother James to go and collect him and bring him back to London. He was not mentally ill at all. He knew his name but nothing else. Don and I brought Tom and his wife Sonia to New Zealand in 1968 and by 1974, when Don and I went to London, Tom and Sonia had moved to Perth, in Australia. I also met Dad in 1974. He was in hospital with emphysema. He gave me an Irish halfpenny. I still have it.

As I finished my book, my last sibling, James, died in London. I am the last one of us left.

It was always on my mind to find Mammy's grave in Aughavale Cemetery in Westport and to put a headstone on it. It took me many years to locate it but I found it in September 2003 when I was in Ireland with my daughter

Margaret and her daughter, Sara. I erected a headstone in 2004 and later Larry and James added their own lovely tributes to Mammy's grave. She is not forgotten and never will be forgotten.

Now it is time to look for Nan's grave in Leigue Cemetery in Ballina.

Me, Granny Noone, and Kit

Me, Margo, and Kit